CULTURE SMART!

HONG KONG

Clare Vickers

·K·U·P·E·R·A·R·D·

First published in Great Britain 2005
by Kuperard, an imprint of Bravo Ltd
59 Hutton Grove, London N12 8DS
Tel: +44 (0) 20 8446 2440   Fax: +44 (0) 20 8446 2441
www.culturesmartguides.com
Inquiries: sales@kuperard.co.uk

Culture Smart! is a registered trademark of Bravo Ltd

Distributed in the United States and Canada
by Random House Distribution Services
1745 Broadway, New York, NY 10019
Tel: +1 (212) 572-2844   Fax: +1 (212) 572-4961
Inquiries: csorders@randomhouse.com

Series Editor Geoffrey Chesler

ISBN-13: 978 1 85733 368 8
ISBN-10: 1 85733 368 3

British Library Cataloguing in Publication Data
A CIP catalogue entry for this book is available from the
British Library

Printed in Malaysia

This book is available for special discounts for bulk purchases for
sales promotions or premiums. Special editions, including
personalized covers, excerpts of existing books, and corporate
imprints, can be created in large quantities for special needs.

For more information in the U.S.A. write to Special
Markets/Premium Sales, 1745 Broadway, MD 6–2, New York,
NY 10019 or e-mail specialmarkets@randomhouse.com.

In the United Kingdom contact Kuperard publishers at the
above address.

Cover image: View from the Peak, Hong Kong Island.
Travel Ink/David Guyler
Brushwork calligraphy on pages 46 and 84 by Bernard Lui

CultureSmart!Consulting and **Culture Smart!** guides have both
contributed to and featured regularly in the weekly travel program
"Fast Track" on BBC World TV.

About the Author

CLARE VICKERS is an English writer who lived in Hong Kong for eighteen years, from 1979 to 1997. Her husband was a member of the Hong Kong Government, and collaborated with her on the history and government chapters of this book as well as other historical books and articles on Hong Kong. She has a degree in modern languages, and has written several dictionaries and textbooks for Hong Kong schools, had a column in the educational section of the *South China Morning Post*, and is the author of *Escape, a Story of Wartime Hong Kong*, written for Hong Kong teenagers. She last worked in the territory in 2004.

Other Books in the Series

- Culture Smart! Argentina
- Culture Smart! Australia
- Culture Smart! Belgium
- Culture Smart! Brazil
- Culture Smart! Britain
- Culture Smart! China
- Culture Smart! Costa Rica
- Culture Smart! Cuba
- Culture Smart! Czech Republic
- Culture Smart! Denmark
- Culture Smart! Finland
- Culture Smart! France
- Culture Smart! Germany
- Culture Smart! Greece
- Culture Smart! Hungary
- Culture Smart! India
- Culture Smart! Ireland
- Culture Smart! Italy
- Culture Smart! Japan
- Culture Smart! Korea
- Culture Smart! Mexico
- Culture Smart! Morocco
- Culture Smart! Netherlands
- Culture Smart! New Zealand
- Culture Smart! Norway
- Culture Smart! Panama
- Culture Smart! Peru
- Culture Smart! Philippines
- Culture Smart! Poland
- Culture Smart! Portugal
- Culture Smart! Russia
- Culture Smart! Singapore
- Culture Smart! Spain
- Culture Smart! Sweden
- Culture Smart! Switzerland
- Culture Smart! Thailand
- Culture Smart! Turkey
- Culture Smart! Ukraine
- Culture Smart! USA
- Culture Smart! Vietnam

Other titles are in preparation. For more information, contact: info@kuperard.co.uk

The publishers would like to thank **CultureSmart!**Consulting for its help in researching and developing the concept for this series.

contents

contents

Map of Hong Kong

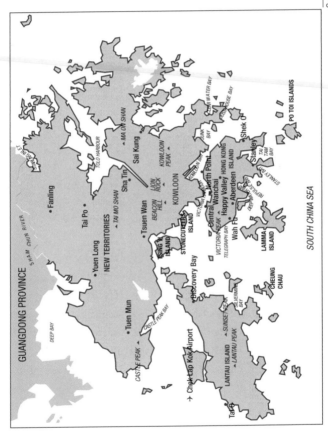

introduction

Hong Kong is unique. Its geography and history
have given it a surprisingly important role in the
world. It is both a primary link for the world to
China and the outpost of the West in the East.

Culturally, Hong Kong is rooted in the traditions
of China, but there is more than a patina of
Westernization. Nearly all the population have
come to the territory in the last hundred years,
most from southern China, but substantial
numbers from the rest of China, from the rest of
Asia, and from beyond. They came to a well-run,
orderly place and found its comparative stability
and the rule of law conducive to the oldest
profession—trade.

Trade is everywhere. In addition to the myriad
shops and stores, street markets and food stalls
operate around the clock. Trade is the lifeblood of
Hong Kong, and talk is the oxygen that fuels it.

The Hong Kong people are many and various.
The substantial majority are Cantonese,
entrepreneurial and industrious people from the
farms and villages of the huge neighboring
province of Guangdong. They brought with them a
varied cuisine that is often acknowledged as "the
best in China," seeing themselves as the French do
in Europe. Their style is open and extroverted

compared to the more dignified and serious northerners. Restaurants and shopping malls overflow with families and groups of friends, talking incessantly and missing no opportunity for a bargain. In the unlikely event that a Hongkonger is alone for a few brief moments, he or she will be talking into a cell phone or listening to a walkman. Silence is not a preferred option.

Taking their style from the Cantonese, other settlers from around the world trade and prosper. There are more holidays in the Hong Kong calendar than in any other place in the world—Chinese, Western, and Indian. And most holidays are celebrated in the streets or in the parks, out with friends, snacking and having fun.

This guide will give you a quick "in" to the multifaceted community and way of life of this vibrant territory. You will find helpful advice on business and meetings, and on social etiquette. You will find the confidence to participate rather than observe. In even a short trip, you can be part of the community life of the Hong Kong people. Private life is a different matter. It is something few outsiders ever share, and it is a real privilege if you do become an insider. In this guide, we hope to give you a few pointers to closer access to it.

Key Facts

Official Name	Hong Kong Special Administrative Region (SAR), China	Cantonese name: *Heung Gong.* Mandarin name: *Xiang Gang*
Main Cities	Hong Kong (Victoria), Kowloon, Tsuen Wan, Shatin	
Area	411.68 sq. miles (1,066.53 sq. km)	
Terrain	Mountainous to hilly, with numerous rocky islands and a natural harbor	
Climate	Tropical monsoon. Cool and humid in winter, hot and rainy from spring through summer, warm and sunny in fall	
Population	Just under 7.5 million	Probably the highest density in the world at 6,250 people per sq. km
Ethnic Makeup	95% Cantonese-speaking Chinese, 5% other	
Average Age	34	
Life Expectancy	81.5 years	
Adult Literacy Rate	92%	
Languages	Written: Chinese and English (official); spoken: Cantonese, Mandarin, some English	
Religion	No official religion: Taoist, Buddhist, 10% Christian, 1% Muslim	
Government	Special administrative region of China with limited democracy	The Head of Government is known as the Chief Executive

Constitution	Hong Kong has its own mini-constitution, called the Basic Law.	The legal system is based on English common law.
Per Capita	GDP $29,000	
Currency	The Hong Kong dollar HK $1 (pegged at roughly 7.8 to US $1) is divided into 100 cents.	Notes are issued in the following denominations: $1,000, $500, $100, $50, $20, $10. Coins are issued as follows: $10, $5, $2, $1, 50c, 20c, and 10c.
Media	The most influential Chinese-language newspapers are *Ming Pao, The Apple Daily,* and *The Oriental Daily.* The main English-language newspapers are *The South China Morning Post* and *The Standard. The Far Eastern Economic Review* is a well-respected weekly magazine.	The government company RTHK produces news and public information programs. There are four commercial TV channels, "Pearl" (English) and "Jade" (Chinese) run by TVB, and "World" (English) and "Home" (Chinese) run by ATV. Cable TV is available. CNN is available on cable. There are 13 radio channels.
Electricity	220 volts, 50 Hz	Transformer needed for 100-v appliances
Telephone	The country code for Hong Kong is 852. Emergency services: 999	
Time	Hong Kong is 8 hours ahead of GMT	

LAND & PEOPLE

TERRAIN

The territory of Hong Kong consists of a peninsula and over two hundred islands, most of which are scarcely more than lone rocks. It is situated near the mouth of the Pearl River, which flows through the province of Guangdong from Guangzhou city (formerly Canton). Central to the territory is Hong Kong Island, facing the Kowloon Peninsula across the harbor. The airport, along with a great deal of new development, is on Lantau, the largest of the islands. Always short of land for building, the Hong Kong government has reclaimed enormous amounts of the shoreline over the years, and the harbor is considerably narrower now than it was fifty years ago.

The whole of the territory is a mere 411.68 square miles (1,066.53 sq. km)—including the sea—but into this small area is packed a population of nearly 7.5 million. The urban districts include some of the densest areas of population on earth, piled into towering skyscrapers that in turn are packed together like books along a shelf. This doesn't look as unattractive as it sounds. In fact, Hong Kong is considered one of the most beautiful of modern cities. The central urban area has a dramatic setting around its deep and busy harbor, and the steep mountains behind it form a grand backdrop to the soaring city blocks.

The main city, formally called Victoria but known locally as Hongkongside, is the oldest colonial settlement. From the nineteenth century it had its cathedral, its governor's residence, government offices, and bank headquarters. It now occupies a strip along the whole north shore of Hong Kong harbor, merging with former villages and dormitory suburbs. Behind Central (the modern business district) rises the Peak, the highest point of Hong Kong Island, into whose steep sides have been inserted perilously narrow skyscrapers. These have some of the most extensive views possible in any city, across the harbor to the

hills separating Hong Kong from the neighboring province of Guangdong.

Opposite the Island, Kowloon extends for miles along the shoreline. Previously the poor relation of the Island, Kowloon boasts few buildings of great age, but it is the center of most of the commerce and has large residential areas. Formerly, small manufacturing enterprises in dingy factory zones were widespread, but in the last ten years the majority of these have moved to mainland China. Imaginatively designed parks, shopping malls, and leisure complexes have been built in their place.

The Ninth Dragon

Where does the name Kowloon come from? Hills are characterized as animals such as dragons or phoenixes. The dragon also signifies the emperor. The name Kowloon is an anglicization of *gau lung*, which means "nine dragons." There were only eight hills guarding the Kowloon peninsula to the north, and a legendary emperor was so upset when he discovered this that he threw himself into the sea. He, being an emperor, had been the ninth, but he had not realized it.

On the Kowloon Peninsula are six other large cities, usually referred to as "new towns," since they were built only in the late 1970s. They are in the area known as the New Territories (see Brief History, below). The new towns, often impressive new developments from previous market towns, are now largely residential, with commercial malls and some industry.

It comes as a surprise to many visitors that Hong Kong combines one of the busiest and buzziest cities on earth with expanses of mountain and sea where you can walk for hours and not meet a soul. There are sandy beaches and secluded woodlands. Stunning views extend around every corner. Outlying islands are comparatively quiet,  and can be quite rural. These areas are designated "country parks," and occupy 40 percent of the landmass of the territory. They are planned to be exempt from new building, although a few encroachments have occurred.

The natural vegetation of the territory is subtropical, with a low scrub of bushes and small trees covering the gentler slopes. Fine old trees still exist in small pockets, but the occasional typhoons have inflicted a great deal of damage to the tallest. Flowering plants and cultivated shrubs do very well, and the parks are full of color.

CLIMATE

The climate is classified as tropical monsoon. From January to April the weather is cool and humid, but it heats up quickly after that and the summer is hot and rainy. The humidity can be quite trying for people from cooler regions, and there is the added annoyance of mosquitoes in some areas. Most buildings and public transportation are air-conditioned, sometimes ferociously, which is a boon in such a crowded place. But by the fall the weather is starting to cool down and dry out, and the best months are October, November, and December, when it is usually clear with sunny days and cool nights.

Average Temperature (Fahrenheit/Celsius)		
	High	**Low**
January	64°/18°	55°/13°
February	63°/17°	55°/13°
March	68°/20°	61°/16°
April	75°/24°	20°/68°
May	82°/28°	75°/24°
June	86°/30°	79°/26°
July	88°/31°	80°/27°
August	88°/31°	80°/27°
September	86°/30°	79°/26°
October	82°/28°	75°/24°
November	75°/24 °	68°/20°
December	66°/19°	60°/15°

Typhoons

The word "typhoon" comes from the Cantonese *dai fung*, which means "big wind." Elsewhere these are called hurricanes or cyclones. Hong Kong often has typhoon warnings, but direct hits are comparatively rare, occurring about once in two years. The warnings are important, and the strength of the typhoon is graded—numbers 1 to 3 are not very significant but next on the list is number 8, and when this is posted, everyone leaves work or school and goes home. After that, a typhoon can go to number 10, extremely strong winds—enough to move parked cars and blow pedestrians over. The sea becomes very rough (ferries are generally cancelled if a number 3 is posted). The actual warnings are shown on public buildings, but most people get their information from TV and radio.

A BRIEF HISTORY

There can be neither safety nor honour for either government until Her Majesty's flag flies on these coasts in a secure position.
(Captain Charles Elliot, 1839)

Hong Kong did not feature in early Chinese history in any special way. A few villages, fishing as well as orthodox agricultural, grew up. The typical

Cantonese shape—walled and square—can still be seen at Kam Tin in the New Territories. Hong Kong's excellent harbor, deep as well as well-protected, was only discovered in the nineteenth century by the British. The name of the whole territory, *Heung Gong* in Cantonese,

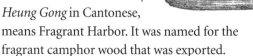

means Fragrant Harbor. It was named for the fragrant camphor wood that was exported.

After the Opium Wars, the Chinese ceded Hong Kong Island to the British. They colonized it as part of the Chuen Pi Treaty (1841), revised by the Treaty of Nanking (August 1842), ending the first Opium War.

The Opium Wars

The two mid-nineteenth-century Opium Wars between Britain and China (Britain joined by France in the second one) were as much about equality and opening up trade with China as about opium. The Manchu Chinese emperors banned their people from importing any goods. Because the Europeans were eager for Chinese exports—porcelain and tea being the most important—an imbalance of trade resulted. Opium, a narcotic, was already smoked in China, but Britain increased the market for it by importing large quantities produced in their colony of India. It was the most profitable product traded in the British Empire at that time. The Chinese Government tried to stamp out both import and consumption, and in 1837 sent a senior official to Canton, the main importing center. Stores of opium were burned, and this became a *casus belli*, justified on Britain's side by its free trade philosophy. Two wars ensued (1839–42 and 1858–60).

The Chinese overestimated their power against the modern war machinery of the West, and were forced into humiliating treaties (now called the Unequal Treaties) establishing privileged rights for foreign traders in newly designated "treaty ports." These treaties were naturally highly resented in China, and because of them Hong Kong's right to a separate existence was always denied by the Chinese government. Of course most treaties are unequal in the sense the Chinese meant, one side being stronger than the other. In hindsight even Chinese historians acknowledge that the treaties benefited many ordinary Chinese people by opening up their country to the modern world. But this did not diminish the importance of Chinese resentment at the existence of Hong Kong and other treaty ports.

"A Barren Island"

Hong Kong was not an obvious prize of the first Opium War. In fact Britain's Foreign Secretary, Palmerston, dubbed it "a barren island with hardly a house upon it," and sacked Charles Elliot, the first governor, and author of the quotation introducing this section, for the weakness of the treaty and the apparent uselessness of Hong Kong.

At that time, Portuguese Macau was the only European town in China, and it traded with China via Canton (Guangzhou), the only city on the south coast, then and now. The Portuguese had been developing Macau as a port since the fifteenth century; but the harbor is shallow, and the Portuguese government did not have the means to make much of its links to its other colonies, such as Goa and Melaka. Hong Kong very quickly replaced it in importance. By 1860, twenty years after the founding of Hong Kong, the head of the British Colonial Office declared it "Another illustration of 'the art of colonization,' . . . and the success is such as to show the flexibility of the present system—or want of system." This was the year in which Kowloon, "long considered a sort of neutral ground" (Governor Davis) and Stonecutters Island, adjacent to it, were added to Hong Kong by the Convention of Peking after the second Opium War.

The area beyond Kowloon, including all the other islands, was not added until 1898. The British wanted this land, which they called the New Territories, to protect the port of Hong Kong and the entrance to the Pearl River from pirates by sea and raids by land. Significantly, it was granted to them (by the Peking Convention) only on a ninety-nine-year lease, which had enormous repercussions in 1997.

The British Empire and Colonies

The British Empire (precursor of the British Commonwealth, a loose organization of states that used to be part of the British Empire) had its origins in the sixteenth and seventeenth centuries. Britain was at that time using its naval traditions to bolster trade and emigration, particularly to North America. India, being the richest and largest colony, was run by the East India Company, but there was a gradual expansion in the eighteenth and nineteenth centuries of ports and land directly controlled by the British government. Other European countries, especially France, fought Britain for possession of, for example, the West Indian sugar-producing islands, but Britain was the major colonial power in the nineteenth and early twentieth centuries when the empire was at its zenith. Its colonies were ruled by governors appointed in London. Initially many had military backgrounds, but gradually a cadre of civilian "colonial officers" was developed. These officers entered through highly competitive exams, being posted between colonies for three to five years at a time. Interestingly, this meritocratic system of preferment by exam was taken from the old Chinese administrative system, which the British greatly admired. India, itself termed an Empire, was governed separately by the Indian Civil Service, which native Indians joined increasingly into the twentieth century, becoming the majority by independence in 1947. From then on, it was only a matter of time until the empire was broken up, and the countries within it became self-governing. Hong Kong was the only colony not to gain full independence.

The Administrative Service
Hong Kong followed the colonial model, with specialist training in written Chinese and spoken Cantonese given to its recruits, known as "cadets." The cadets had the benefit of at least one posting in another colony, as well as four or five promotions through the ranks in Hong Kong. Local Chinese joined the Administrative Service, as it was called, later than elsewhere, but by 1997 constituted the majority of the total of four hundred. Half the expatriate Administrative Officers left in 1997, but the service remains the fundamental elite of

government with entry by a tough competitive exam, interview, and group tests, three thousand graduates applying every year for thirty places. Thus the colonial system of government continues uniquely under China's Communist regime.

By 1898, Hong Kong had become one of the leading ports in Asia and one of the most successful colonies in the British Empire. There was a considerable exodus from Hong Kong and Guangdong at this time to Australia, the United States, and the Straits Settlements (today's Malaysia). The recruitment and dispatch of migrants was one of the major activities of Hong Kong in the nineteenth century.

Hong Kong had diversified while continuing to grow as an entrepôt to China. But still it lagged behind Shanghai, which was better placed, in the middle of the eastern coast. Shanghai was less strictly controlled by the Colonial Office, with an "International Settlement" government led by expatriate businessmen. Hong Kong was the quieter center right through to the absorption of Shanghai into China in 1949. Its growth socially as well as economically was steady, however. Missionary societies such as the London Missionary Society and the Morrison Education Society developed education that was vital for providing the junior members of the government as well as more widely filling the gaps in middle management in the substantial local businesses that had developed, such as Jardine Matheson and John Swire.

Colonial Governors

Hong Kong was governed during its 150 years of British rule by governors sent out from Britain. Many had had experience in other colonies, such as Malaya, the West Indies, or Ceylon.

Sir John Bowring (1854–9) was a scholar in Chinese but not a good administrator. It was in his governorship that the greatest threat to British rule occurred, in January 1857. Cleverly assuming that only the European expatriates ate bread, criminals poured arsenic into the bread dough being made at the E-sing Bakery, the most popular of the Hong Kong bakers. Only because too much, too noticeable, and too nauseating an amount of arsenic was put in did the move fail, and nobody died. Five hundred men were arrested and 160 were transported back to China, and there were demands for execution without trial. However, the true culprits were never found.

Sir John Pope-Hennessy (1877–82) was a colorful Irish governor, renowned for liberal views and a quick temper. He was an intelligent man, and notably pro-Chinese, making himself very unpopular with the expatriate community for promoting Chinese in the political system. Ng Choy, the Chinese man he appointed as the first on the Legislative Council in 1880, lasted only until 1883, when he was involved in a speculation craze and went bankrupt. Hennessy found himself in a dilemma over backing sanitary measures that put a burden on the Chinese community but which were necessary for health. He also opposed traditional girl-child (*mooi jai*) domestic slavery and helped with the establishment of the Po Leung Kuk ("Protect the Innocents" Society), which made him unpopular with many from the more affluent section of Chinese society. Hennessy's hasty temper was his downfall. He surprised his wife and a judge in her boudoir, looking at a catalog of nude statues from an Italian museum. This circumstantial evidence of improper behavior led him to attack the judge in the street with his umbrella! Hennessy left Hong Kong shortly afterward to become Governor of Mauritius.

Sir Cecil Clementi (1925–30) was the first governor to have started his career in Hong Kong. He was active in fostering education. Among his varied personal achievements he published erotic Latin verse and walked three thousand miles from Central Asia to Kowloon. He went on to become governor of the most dynamic colony of the time, the Straits Settlements (Malaysia).

Sir Murray Maclehose (1971–82) was governor during the period of Hong Kong's greatest expansion and development. He inherited a colony whose reputation for corruption, especially in the police force, was legendary, and in 1974 founded the Independent Commission Against Corruption (ICAC), which had wide-ranging powers, including the ability to investigate any government servant who appeared to be living above his means. Its effectiveness led to Hong Kong becoming one of the least corrupt societies in the world, and serving as a model to other governments wishing to improve their own reputation in this regard, in places as diverse as Taiwan, Peru, and New South Wales. He was a committed environmentalist, and a 62-mile (100-km) walking path in the New Territories is named the Maclehose Trail after him. Maclehose initiated the talks on the future of Hong Kong with the mainland government, paving the way for the handover to China in 1997.

Chris Patten (1992–7) was the only governor to refuse a knighthood. He had been a senior Conservative politician in England who lost his seat in a general election and was compensated by being given the governorship of Hong Kong. He was therefore an enthusiastic democrat, which resulted in clashes with the mainland government during the vital five years before the handover of Hong Kong; but his democratic style endeared him to local people, and he was often seen with his family in public places.

However, there was a noticeable gap generally in

society between the Chinese and the expatriates: "It is extraordinary—not to say discreditable—that after fifty-five years of British rule, the vast majority of Chinese in Hong Kong should remain so little anglicized." (Governor Hercules Robinson, 1895). Some of this non-anglicization was deliberate, and related to legislation demanded by the expatriates for segregation via different house-type—European housing and Chinese housing. The main example of this segregation was the Peak, the mountain in the center of Hong Kong Island, which was reserved for, and is still dominated by, European housing.

Some segregation was caused not by racism but by understandable medical concerns about the spread of disease. Malaria and other fevers were widespread, and even today many of the world's major epidemics start in southern China, where people and animals live in close proximity.

In general Hong Kong was well and fairly, if not democratically, governed. There were problems that defeated the government, one being the Triad societies, organized criminal gangs with pseudo-religious rules that still exist today.

Triads

Triads are the world's biggest organized crime group. Their origin lies in the resistance to the Mongol invasion and conquest of China in the thirteenth century. They were an underground force that overstayed its welcome when the Han Chinese retook power under the Ming dynasty. They developed their own language for coded communication and religious ceremony. As in organized crime elsewhere, they were involved in controlling illegal gambling and prostitution. There were an estimated fifteen thousand Triads in the late nineteenth century when an attempt to make membership of a Triad society punishable by branding was vetoed by the British home government. In the 1950s they became involved in illegal immigration, and controlled various trades such as the interior decoration of the new housing estates. They operated through intimidation, most dangerously linked through some members in the police. By the end of the twentieth century the police had managed to wipe out Triads from their ranks, and the takeover by the mainland, where the elimination of Triads had been one success of early Communist rule, lessened the evil generally.

The Dilemma of Democracy
The question of democratization was another classic dilemma, too much even for governors with democratic or pro-Chinese instincts such as Pope-Hennessy.

Nevertheless, the movements in China for a

less autocratic government highlighted Hong Kong's relative liberalism compared to the mainland. In 1899, "It was assumed that the knowledge of the just treatment of the Chinese inhabitants of Hong Kong and British Kowloon would induce the population of the leased area (the New Territories) to accept the jurisdiction of Great Britain with equanimity if not with pleasure." This was Governor Henry Blake on the takeover of the New Territories. In fact there was some physical resistance by the local leadership, especially the Tang clan of Tai Po and Yuen Long villages, because they were proudly Chinese and quite contented with their agricultural lifestyle rather than the unequal society of the British colony. The New Territories were lightly governed, and were used as a buffer zone against immigration as much as militarily, and they were not developed until the 1970s.

Nearer to the heart of Hong Kong, there was long-term argument about Kowloon Walled City, a village in the north of the Kowloon peninsula that had been used as the local Chinese officials' ("Mandarins") base next to Hong Kong and about which the treaty regarding the takeover of the New Territories was vague. It was not actually governed by the British until the 1980s, and it meanwhile became a notorious refuge for criminals escaping the police.

KOWLOON WALLED CITY

The original Walled City was a nineteenth-century fort built on the site of an earlier military post. It was in the area negotiated in the Peking Convention. The Chinese authorities decided to hold on to it as a reminder of China's presence and proximity to British Hong Kong.

The Peking Convention excluded the Walled City, which had an estimated population of seven hundred. The British conceded that China could keep troops there as long as they did not interfere with the government of the colony. Britain quickly went back on this informal promise, attacking the fort in 1899, only to find it deserted. Nothing further was done, and it was left to itself.

During the Second World War, the Japanese demolished much of the City to acquire building materials for the nearby airport. After the war, and with an influx of immigrants from China, squatters took over and it became a haven for criminals and drug addicts, as the Hong Kong Police had no right of entry. There was a murder in 1959 that caused a diplomatic incident. Neither Britain nor China wanted to take responsibility for this part of the territory.

The Triads ruled the roost until the mid-1970s, when a police crackdown in the main area of Kowloon diminished their numbers and power. The Walled City, not subject to the health and building regulations of the rest of Hong Kong, was then built up into an unsafe and unsanitary jumble of high-rise blocks. Eventually the whole Walled City was one vast block, covering well over six acres (0.026 sq. km), the only open area being a courtyard containing a revered but stunted tree. Eight water pipes and miles of illegal electricity cables and gas pipes provided services.

By the 1980s, the City had a population estimated at an incredible fifty thousand, and a crime rate far below the Hong Kong average, despite the notable lack of any law enforcement. It was home to hundreds of medical practitioners who had none of the qualifications necessary to work in Hong Kong itself—notably bonesetters and tooth pullers. Many local Chinese, even those educated in a Western style, would consult these physicians right up until the City was demolished.

In 1993, the whole tottering edifice was destroyed, but not before a Jackie Chan movie, *Crime Story*, was made using the deserted interior, with its maze of dark passages lined with rubbish and wildly looped cables.

The area has now been turned into Kowloon Walled City Park, which seeks to preserve the original character of the City. It is designed to resemble a Qing Dynasty garden, with the centerpiece being a *yamen*, or hall, which houses a photographic exhibition.

The Early Twentieth Century

The pressure for Britain to take the New Territories came from the international strategic concerns at Russian and French expansion in Asia. The international tension continued until the defeat of the Russians by the Japanese in 1905 and the new alliance of the British with the French, the Entente Cordiale, of the same year.

By this time Chinese events were making a significant impact on Hong Kong. The desire not to come into conflict with the Chinese government led to the expulsion in 1896 of one of the leaders of revolt against the Manchu rule—Sun Yat-sen, who had been educated as a doctor in Hong Kong. After his expulsion there was sympathy for his cause, and in the next such case to be discussed, that of the liberal reformer Kang Yu-wei, the decision went the other way: he was given refuge when his revolution failed after a hundred days in 1900. In 1911 the revolution led by Sun Yat-sen had initial success, but it took a long time, until 1928–9, to cover the whole of China, and from then on the Japanese were threatening from the east, starting with the seizure of Manchuria in 1931 and Shanghai in 1932.

Sun Yat-sen came back to Hong Kong as President of China to speak at the university congregation in 1923. He spoke out in appreciation of Hong Kong and British colonialism:

"Afterwards [after his medical training in Hong Kong] I saw the outside world, and I began to wonder how it was that foreigners, that Englishmen could do such things as they had done, for example with the barren rock of Hong Kong."

Hong Kong was struggling a bit in the interwar period, with the decline of Britain and its doctrine of free trade. In 1931 Britain was forced off the gold standard by economic circumstances, and on to a system of imperial preferences, a protectionist policy based on imperial connections. This did not suit Hong Kong, which was more a free trader in and out of China than a producer of anything.

Japanese Occupation

During the 1930s, the dominance of Japan assumed paramount importance in both China and Hong Kong. This became a real threat once the war with Germany began in 1939, because Japan was allied to Germany under the Axis Pact (1936). However, there were still many British in Hong Kong who underestimated the Japanese, because of their physical stature, lack of sporting ability, and nationalistic immaturity. It came as a complete surprise, therefore, when, in the early hours of

December 8, 1941, and simultaneously with Pearl Harbor, Hong Kong was attacked. The Japanese quickly overran the New Territories—the newly built Gin Drinkers fortified line had to be abandoned for lack of troops. Next came Kai Tak airstrip and the catastrophic sinking of the two battleships,  *Prince of Wales* and *Repulse*, on their way from Singapore to help.

Kowloon fell in five days but the governor, Sir Mark Young, rejected surrender. The Japanese then landed on the middle of the island on December 18, advancing quickly over it to Repulse Bay, and forced a surrender on Christmas Day after a Japanese ultimatum wishing the British troops a happy Christmas!

The treatment of military prisoners and expatriate civilians, who were put in the same camps, was bad, as Japanese culture did not honor surrender. Many died of starvation or ill-treatment. The Japanese also oppressed the local population, and the majority were forced by lack of food to move back across the border, bringing the population down from 1,600,000 to 600,000.

It was a ragged territory, the object of American bombing against the Japanese, that emerged from this occupation on August 30, 1945, with the arrival of the British Pacific fleet.

Postwar Developments

It was lucky for British Hong Kong that it was not the American fleet that got there first. The Americans were a real threat to Hong Kong as a British colony: President Roosevelt believed that the self-determination clause in the Atlantic Charter (the forerunner to the UN Charter) applied to British colonies as much as to German, Italian, and Japanese ones. He pressed for Hong Kong to be given to Chiang Kai Shek's China. However, Churchill, strong on the British Empire, hung on to it.

Nevertheless it was a new world that Hong Kong faced after the war, and the Labour Government that replaced Churchill's wartime coalition was not enthusiastic about the Empire, wishing to bring Hong Kong up-to-date in terms of democratic government. The governor, Sir Mark Young (1941–7), who had been imprisoned in Japan in the war, was strongly in favor of some measure of democratization, and announced his views on his return. A measure, called the Young Plan, was approved by London. This ensured the legislature would be half elected by the Chinese population and half by the foreign population.

This was not enough for some, but the reason it was not followed up in the next governorship, that of Sir Alexander Grantham (1947–57), was ironically the changes in China—the civil war between Chiang Kai Shek's Nationalist Government and the Communists under Mao Tse-tung (Mao Zedong). The violent takeover by Communism in 1949 and the survival of a highly armed Nationalist Taiwan worried the leaders of the local community in Hong Kong, who feared that elections would be taken over by these two extremes. They asked that the Young Plan be postponed.

Events in China affected Hong Kong in a more direct way—there was an enormous influx of refugees, which doubled the population in five years. A major fire on Christmas Day, 1953, in one of the squatter areas that had grown up around the city, caused a big policy change. The biggest public housing program in the world was launched. It housed as much as half the population within the next thirty years.

The new population provided cheap labor for the transformation of Hong Kong from an entrepôt port into a manufacturing center, providing cheap goods such as toys, wigs, and textiles to undercut rivals such as Britain and other rich countries. Indeed the rapid development of Hong Kong put it on a level with Britain in GDP per head by the late 1980s.

Thirty people a day were "legally" entering Hong Kong during this time, and as many as a hundred illegally. Hong Kong may have been the only place in the world where the legitimate incoming population was chosen not by its own government but by the "exporting" country, China. Continuing immigration necessitated a great deal of social provision in the latter half of the twentieth century, when standards of health, housing, and education were usually compared to Britain's rather than to China's.

Politically there was still no change in favor of democracy because of fear of the continuing extremism and instability across the border overflowing into Hong Kong. Mao Zedong in fact left Hong Kong alone, even when the anarchy of the Cultural Revolution spread to the colony in 1967. There were riots, and some policemen and rioters were killed. It was said that Mao and in particular his pragmatic deputy, Chou En-lai (Zhou Enlai), saw the continuance of Hong Kong as a useful outlet for Chinese goods and an equally useful entrance for imports.

The Handover

While China had recovered from the Cultural Revolution by the end of the 1970s under the newly pragmatic leadership of Deng Xiaoping, it was the British side that felt it had to change things in a major way. In 1983 Prime Minister Margaret Thatcher began formal negotiations with Deng on the future of Hong Kong because of the approaching expiry of the ninety-nine-year lease on the New Territories. Thatcher wanted to negotiate for the return of only the New Territories, as stated by the agreement, but was told that they could not be separated. Reservoirs and new towns had been built there, and Hong Kong Island and Kowloon were not viable without them. So she caved in (uniquely?) and the whole territory of Hong Kong was promised back to China by the Joint Declaration of 1984. In Beijing to sign the document, Thatcher tripped on the steps of the Great Hall of the People, symbolizing to the Chinese either British disarray or merely "bad joss" (the fates against them). The Joint Declaration promised that Hong Kong would retain its system and autonomy, under Deng's slogan, "one country, two systems."

It had been thought too dangerous to institute self-government before the future was clarified—China was less threatened by a colony than by a democracy. Even though all other colonies were given independence from Britain by the 1980s, Hong Kong therefore had to make do with a partial (district-level) democracy at first. Even when the Legislative Council was democratized after the Joint Declaration, it did not have the crucial power of choosing the Governor's Executive Council, which remained appointed by the Governor through the transfer to China in 1997 and beyond under the Chief Executive.

Although democratic elements in Hong Kong, such as the Democratic Party led by Martin Lee, and independents like Christine Loh, were not happy with the semi-democracy provided at China's insistence, they acknowledged that it ensured a stable and prosperous transfer of power from Britain to China in 1997 and in the early years of Chinese rule.

This transfer of power went smoothly, a lot more so than had been expected eight years before. In 1989, events in China affected Hong Kong as never before or since. A major student-led movement in China arguing for democracy and against corruption was crushed by military means in Tiananmen Square, Beijing. Hong Kong people, to the tune of an estimated two million, came out into the streets in protest. Fears of what would happen in Hong Kong when it was absorbed into China led to increased emigration, particularly of liberal middle-class residents. Half the remaining expatriates in the Administrative Service, for example, who were fully entitled to stay, left before 1997 largely for reasons of concern over the post-1997 political prospects.

On June 30, 1997, the handover of Hong Kong to the People's Republic of China officially took place. A short ceremony was held at the Hong Kong Convention Centre. Prince Charles,

representing the Queen, and the Chinese President
Jiang Zemin made speeches, and the British and
colonial Hong Kong flags were lowered. Just after
midnight on July 1, the Chinese flag and the Hong
Kong Special Administrative Region
flag (a bauhinia flower in white
on a red background) were raised.
Hong Kong is now officially
known as Hong Kong (SAR).

Since the Handover
As it turned out, China was very careful in the first
years of sovereignty not to break the Joint
Declaration or interfere with the status quo. This
was a tribute to the mainland's pragmatism
inherited from Deng; to the balancing role played
by the first Chief Executive (the old position of
Governor); and to the firmly defensive position of
Anson Chan, the Chief Secretary (head of the civil
service and deputy to the Chief Executive)
appointed by the last Governor, Chris Patten.

Ironically, Hong Kong has had few problems
where they were most expected, in the political
arena, and most in economics, which had been
predicted to go smoothly. The downturn was a
regional rather than a specific problem, but it has
been exacerbated by the marginalizing of Hong
Kong as a business center now that China, with
much cheaper labor and a somewhat casual

attitude toward health, safety, and environmental regulations, has become a major player in the commercial and financial world.

Tung Chee-hwa, the first Chief Executive of Hong Kong Special Autonomous Region, came to Hong Kong from war-torn Shanghai with his family when he was ten years old. He went to a British university and spent time in America, and had been in business for the thirty years before his appointment. He was a generally acceptable choice of leader, apolitical, and somewhat scholarly. He tends to foster the image of "Uncle Tung." Critics complain that he has done nothing positive in his tenure; it is difficult to see what he could do with the Beijing government towering in the background.

Despite the fear of China, Hong Kong people have shown themselves relatively robust politically, continuing to elect democrats to the Legislature.

A proposed law to penalize "crimes against the state" made hundreds of thousands of Hong Kong people come out in protest in July 2003, blocking streets for six and a half hours. According to one protester, the law was so wide-ranging that anything could be punished. The march against the anti-subversion legislation eclipsed ceremonies marking the 1997 handover to China. Chief Executive Tung gave assurances that his government would continue to take active steps to maintain and

safeguard rights and freedoms. By September the
bill had been withdrawn in order that it be
rewritten in a way that was more acceptable.

The key moment may be in 2006, when, as
promised by the Joint Declaration, there will be a
direct election for the successor to Tung.

THE PEOPLE OF HONG KONG
The Cantonese

Almost all the population of Hong Kong are
Cantonese (*Guangdong yan*), named for the
province of Guangdong. The Cantonese are one of
the dozen or so main
ethnic and linguistic
groups in China. They
belong to the dominant
major group
(constituting the large
star of the five on the
national flag), the Han

Chinese. You may sometimes see them called *boon
dei* or *punti*, which just means "locals."

The Cantonese, like many southerners in the
northern hemisphere, were generally smaller and
browner than more northerly Han Chinese, who
occupy the center and northeast of the country.
Their diet of rice has contributed to the smaller
body size, and they are becoming larger and fatter

with the advent of other staples, notably wheat-based food such as bread.

The Cantonese have a reputation among their compatriots for shrewdness and business sense. With the huge success of Hong Kong in the last fifty years, this reputation has grown in the world at large. Along with the Shanghainese, they dominate business in China.

Northern Chinese also tend to regard the Cantonese as unintellectual, loud, and overexcited in public, much as northern Europeans have traditionally viewed the excitable Mediterranean peoples. Certainly if you walk into a Hong Kong restaurant you will find the decibel level extreme, and looking around at the animated faces, in parties of friends and families, all talking at the tops of their voices, you might wonder who ever thought that Orientals were inscrutable.

The Cantonese are also famed within China for their food, and their willingness to eat anything "that turns its back to heaven." Because of the history of Hong Kong, the Cantonese constitute the largest percentage of Chinese that you will find in other countries, particularly the British Commonwealth and America.

The Hakka

The Hakka are not now a very distinguishable minority of the population of Hong Kong, but their origins are not Cantonese and they were until recently a distinctly poorer, rural group, sometimes even characterized as gypsies. They had migrated from central to southern China in various waves to escape, for example, the Mongolian and Manchurian invasions and other earlier ethnic pressures.

The term "Hakka" was not originally a designation for a different ethnic group living in a particular area, but indicative of their status as "guests" who had left their homelands, in contrast to residents originally from the area. They later acquired the nickname "Jews of Asia," reflecting these mass migrations and the Hakkas' pioneering spirit. They also have a certain heroic quality in Chinese history: they are said to have escorted the Song royal household as it fled the Mongolians to Guangdong and fought bravely and died courageously in battles with the Mongolian armies. There are many Hakka among the overseas Chinese in the region and an estimated three million in Taiwan.

The Rest
About 3 percent of the population are neither Cantonese nor Hakka. This includes about 2 percent who are other Chinese groups, including northerners, Shanghainese, and in particular Chiu Chow, a group from just up the coast (and therefore sometimes defined as Cantonese) who

are known as hard workers and drinkers of strong oolong tea.

Expatriates from all over the world are found in many professional and business areas, and number about half a million. In one international secondary school it was estimated that the children came from over eighty different ethnic groups.

An important minority is that from the Indian subcontinent. This group is more integrated than the Westerners, many of the younger members speaking fluent Cantonese, but at the same time it suffers more racial discrimination from the Chinese, in part because of color. The Indians rival the Cantonese in business ability, importing from the subcontinent and trading in the region. Most of the successful Indian businesspeople are Hindus from the province of Sindh, now in Pakistan. After independence, the Hindu community moved mainly to Mumbai (Bombay) and thence to the rest of the world. You can often recognize a Sindhi because many of their surnames end in —ani. The Sindhis are big in import-export, notably clothing and textiles. Their extensive families spread around the world, and tend to intermarry, making ever-larger business networks.

There are also Sikhs, many of whom are descended from those brought in as police by the British, who knew the fear that a bearded, heavy-set giant of a man with a fearsome expression could inspire in the comparatively small and beardless Cantonese. There are Pakistanis, whose ancestors were also traders or police. During the past ten or twenty years professionals from the Indian subcontinent have come into Hong Kong as educators and specialists.

Filipino and Thai workers also have a distinctive presence in the territory. The women are popular "domestic helpers" with Chinese and expatriate families alike.

LANGUAGES

The official languages of Hong Kong are Chinese and English. The word "Chinese" refers to the written language, which is the same wherever you go in China. Each character is like a picture of the word it represents. You will often see people sketching characters on their hands with their fingers when trying to explain a word to a person from another dialect group. This common script is extremely useful in a huge country like China, and serves to unify the people more than any other cultural feature. However, the script has some variations, as mainland China adopted a simplified script that is not generally understood in

清

Hong Kong or Taiwan. Only some characters are simplified. Singapore has also simplified its script, but in different ways.

While the variations in written Chinese are not great, the way in which the words are spoken varies considerably. Mandarin or Putonghua (*pu tong wa* in Cantonese) means "common language," and it is the official spoken language of China, based on the Beijing dialect. Cantonese is the variant spoken in Hong Kong and over the border in Guangdong province. An example of the difference is that "Beijing" is the Mandarin pronunciation, and "Pak-king" the Cantonese—which is why the British called it Peking.

Cantonese

Perhaps the clearest evidence that Cantonese is the closest language to ancient Chinese is that classical Chinese poetry is pronounced closest to its meaning in Cantonese. However, this should not be taken to imply that the Cantonese are generally literature lovers or intellectuals: in fact the Cantonese, and especially those in Hong Kong, have a reputation for being "peasants" with a more materialistic than intellectual approach to life compared to the people of the north and east.

About 98 percent of the population speak Cantonese—*Guangdong wa*—as their mother tongue. It is also the language of most of the popular films from the 1970s onward, notably *kung fu* movies, and has its own pop music, called Cantopop. Cantonese is a tonal language. The intonation or "song" you use when speaking varies according to the word and not according to your mood or the emphasis you want in that sentence. Cantonese has more tones than any other Chinese language, which makes it especially hard for a foreigner to learn. If you get the tones wrong, a Cantonese speaker will literally not understand you. The words will either be meaningless or mean something completely different, which can be very embarrassing! Emphasis is provided by additional words, usually "particles" used at the end of sentences. As a general rule, the less-educated speakers use more emphatic particles, and since many of these end in "—*aa*," there is a certain sound that is uniquely Cantonese.

Cantonese is regarded as a dialect, although there is evidence that the spoken Chinese of the Tang Dynasty (618–906 CE) was closer to Cantonese than Mandarin, or *pu tong wa*. The reason for this is the historical recurrence of China's being attacked from the north, thus pushing the defeated existing leaders south as far as Guangdong Province. Both the Sung Dynasty leaders in the thirteenth century and the Ming Dynasty leaders in the sixteenth century followed this pattern of exile.

Mandarin is widely taught in Hong Kong, and local businesspeople find they need it for any trade that involves more than Guangdong Province.

Other Chinese Dialects

As well as these two forms of the spoken language, other Chinese dialects can be heard, notably that from Shanghai, where many immigrants came from in the 1950s. In Shanghainese there are some sounds that are not found in any other Chinese dialect, so you may notice that it sounds different from Cantonese. It also has its own words and phrases. Taiwanese and Hokkienese from Fujian province are also heard. Like Cantonese, they tend to have more richness and color than an official language such as Mandarin.

English is the preferred language of business between non-Chinese, or between Chinese and other groups. The sizeable Indian population are mostly from Sindh, and speak Sindhi at home, but their English is fluent and they are usually educated at English-speaking schools. Many Japanese and Korean businesspeople live in Hong Kong, and there is a Japanese school. Likewise, the French and German speakers have their own schools.

A Bilingual Society?

You might think that Hong Kong would be the ideal bilingual society. Street signs and government forms are presented in English and Chinese, and both languages are highly visible. Yet it has been shown that if two languages are used so extensively, there will be two monolingual cultures. There is no call for Chinese to read English, or vice versa. Visitors often compare the English of Hongkongers unfavorably with the rest of China. For a language to succeed, it has to be useful, and for most Hongkongers, English is only marginally useful.

MTR Names

Originally, several of the MTR (mass transit railway) stations had names that were different in English and Chinese. Yau Ma Tei was Waterloo because it was on the corner of Waterloo Road, Mong Kok was Argyle for a similar reason. But this caused confusion because local people didn't know where Waterloo or Argyle Stations were, and English speakers had never heard of Yau Ma Tei and Mong Kok. Eventually the Chinese names prevailed. Strangely, Mong Kok was originally Wong Kok in Cantonese: apparently the man hanging the sign turned the W upside down!

GOVERNMENT AND POLITICS

The present government of the Hong Kong Special Administrative Region is in the hands of the Hong Kong business establishment, fully endorsed by the Chinese government. It is not an elected government: it has been appointed by China in several stages at different times, and is not very different from the system brought in by the British.

The business of government is done by career administrators (Administrative Officers, or AOs) who are responsible for thinking up, initiating, and putting into practice government policies. Executive Officers (EOs) are responsible for enacting the policies and managing them. They are supported by clerical and technical staff. It is a lean government, with comparatively few bureaucrats as a proportion of the population.

The government is led by the Chief Executive (formerly the Governor), who presides over the Chief Secretary (head of the Administrative Service), the Secretary for Justice (head of the Judiciary), and the Financial Secretary.

AOs have a lot more power than they would in a democracy, but this is shaped and checked by the politicians who make up the Legislative Council. The makeup of Legco (pronounced "Ledge-co") has varied over the years, but despite efforts in the 1990s, notably by Chris

Patten, to democratize further, it remains a body whose members are not directly elected. As in the mainland, elections are restricted, and the candidates are chosen largely by the administration. Legco comprises sixty members, with twenty-four members returned by geographical constituencies through direct elections, six members by an Election Committee, and thirty members by functional constituencies. These functional constituencies were created by dividing the population (but not all of it) into areas of expertise or influence, such as education, labor, or law. On a local level, each of the eighteen districts of Hong Kong has a District Office (AOs and EOs) and a District Board (elected).

In practice, there is comparatively little politics in Hong Kong. The media and some of the Legco members are not uncritical of the administration, but compared to the space and effort devoted to political matters seen in democratic countries, there is little debate. Whether this comes from apathy or the tendency of Hongkongers to keep a prudent silence on matters controversial, it is hard to say. A book of cartoons by American cartoonist Larry Feign, published in 1997, had the title *Let's All Shut Up and Make Money*, and that seems to sum up the typical Hong Kong attitude.

HONG KONG'S PLACE IN THE REGION

Hong Kong was important in the last half of the twentieth century for being the gateway to China. Goods and people streamed through the port and airport in both directions, leaving a thin film of money in Hong Kong on every trip. This role has of course largely declined since the rest of China has opened up to trade and tourism. However, Hong Kong still has three main roles in the region.

One is that of the acceptable face of modern China. This is a recent role, post-1997, and links with the main propaganda line, that it is not "just another Chinese city." Its rule of law, social equality, and welfare stand out against successful but more corrupt and harsh regimes around it. It offers traditional Chinese culture in a way that the mainland is only just reviving, as well as a cosmopolitan center for business and tourism.

The second role is as one of the semi-democratic but successful southeast Asian nations that were known in the 1990s as the "four little dragons"—Hong Kong, Singapore, South Korea, and Taiwan—the big dragons being China and Japan. Countries like Malaysia and Thailand look to Hong Kong (though they might not admit it) as a model of a place that has achieved social harmony with prosperity. Hong Kong's one big rival in the region is Singapore—independent and democratic, but with a reputation for an unnecessarily tough government and a sanitized style of life. Singapore has traditionally seen Hong Kong as corrupt (which it was, until the 1980s), too obsessed with money, and dissolute. The Cantonese film industry has done little to modify these beliefs. By contrast, Hongkongers think of the Singaporeans as lazy, not properly Chinese, and boring.

The third role is Hong Kong's special relationship with Taiwan. China still does not acknowledge the autonomy of Taiwan, and indeed threatens it with invasion if independence is declared. Official links therefore between the two countries are almost nonexistent, and Taiwan is isolated internationally by Chinese diplomatic pressure. However, Hong Kong has always had better relationships with Taiwan, and has been in practice allowed by China to continue these. This is beneficial economically. For example, all travel between Taiwan and China has to come through Hong Kong. The future of Taiwan is uncertain. It is possible that political pressure from within will push it to independence despite Chinese threats: it has a big army, and support and arms from the U.S.A. However, it is more likely that the present anomaly by which Taiwan on the one side claims it is the only legitimate government of China, and China on the other denies its separate existence, will continue to operate in the present pragmatic and remarkably successful way. Taiwan continues to prosper, and there is much "unofficial" Taiwanese investment in China, again much of it brokered in Hong Kong, which benefits Hong Kong both directly and in terms of its political usefulness to China and Taiwan alike.

chapter two

VALUES & ATTITUDES

THE CHINESE WAY

The Hong Kong Chinese are proud of being Chinese, and most of their customs are very similar to those of the mainland. But 150 years of British rule did influence them, and the trade-linked prosperity of the last thirty years has Westernized them.

To outsiders, Hong Kong seems to epitomize middle-class life. For the most part, people are well-dressed, soberly behaved, and industrious, and believe in the "bourgeois" values of education, hard work, and providing for the family. It is difficult to tease out the strands of traditional Chinese from those of traditional Western attitudes, since they have much in common.

Much social behavior both within the family and outside has come down from Confucius, the Chinese sage of the sixth century BCE. Confucius was an idealist, who taught the importance of social order and justice. It was very important to him that rulers should behave as rulers should, their people as peoples should, fathers as fathers, sons as sons. This has led to the strong element in Chinese behavior of obedience and conservatism. Filial piety is a peculiarly Chinese term, and refers not only to the pious deference of a son to a father but also of the employee to the boss, the person below to the person above in all dealings. When the Hong Kong delegation negotiating the handover agreement went to Beijing, they were openly told that their correct attitude would be that of a son craving indulgence from a father.

Behavior toward bosses is therefore different from that of most cultures. There is much more quiet acceptance, especially in front of others, and a general desire not to offend, even at the price of truth. For example, a definite statement made on a political point will be agreed with, whatever the private feelings.

The more aggressive and egalitarian behavior of Westerners is tolerated and has had some influence in Hong Kong, but it is still better for foreigners to be aware of the primacy of social harmony in their dealings with the Hong Kong Chinese. Arguments are taboo, even sometimes in academic circles where debate is assumed to be normal in most societies. In a survey of the importance of certain virtues in the workplace, nearly all Hong Kong office workers ranked harmony well above hard work, efficiency, attention to detail, and honesty.

As can be seen from the sections on *feng shui* and astrology (see Chapter 3), the courtship of Lady Luck and the thwarting of evil spirits influence much of everyday life. Young people have not generally rebelled against the traditions that go with this—wearing new clothes at Chinese New Year,

sweeping the grandparents' graves at Ching Ming, and doing what is deemed necessary for luck in business ventures.

Foreigners will find that a casual attitude to invitations is not usual among the Chinese in Hong Kong. There is an ingrained desire not to feel obliged to someone. This means that there is no tradition of informal entertaining such as exist in many other cultures. It is not normally done to invite people in a spirit of equality to the home, expecting casual clothing and perhaps a modest bottle of wine or bunch of flowers, and providing a two- or three-course meal or barbecue. If they are invited for dinner they will tend to bring, for example, a bottle of whiskey, not a bottle of wine, and may expect a feast in return. Generally, the invitation would come only from a superior to an inferior, which reinforces this feeling of obligation, so the bringing of an extravagant present will remove the social obligation that would otherwise result from being invited into someone's home for a meal.

Certain attitudes are regarded by the Chinese as foreign, and therefore undesirable. There is little tolerance of extravagant or unusual lifestyles or behavior, although in practice the Chinese will not be overt in their disapproval, so it may go unnoticed by the foreigner. Certain public conduct that is generally tolerated in Western culture is disapproved of by Hongkongers. This includes kissing and displays of intimacy, especially among gays, losing one's temper, and wearing outlandish or inappropriate clothes—in fact, anything extreme.

By contrast, much social behavior that foreigners would condemn may be tolerated, or is even the norm among the Chinese. This includes speaking to strangers in an abrupt and "no-frills" way (which may, to a foreigner, seem rude); laughing when someone falls over in the street, or is otherwise hurt (laughter covers embarrassment and indecision about what to do); mocking and criticizing a foreigner's attempts to speak Chinese; carrying on loud conversations on cell phones; hawking and spitting in the street (this is now much less common than it was); and having general disregard for the environment. All these aspects of everyday Chinese behavior are sources of irritation for many visitors.

THE LEGACY OF THE BRITISH

Many of the institutions of Hong Kong are British in origin or in inspiration. The civil service in particular, having been designed and run by the British for 150 years, continues to operate in a British style. The same applies to the style and traditions in big business, especially in the top "hongs" or large business firms, led by "taipans," or big businessmen. Well-known hongs include Swires (which owns Cathay Pacific, the Hong Kong airline), Jardine Matheson, and HSBC, the Hong Kong and Shanghai Banking Corporation, headquartered in Hong Kong. They are essentially Western with small elements of Chinese tradition such as paying a thirteenth month of wages or employing a *feng shui* expert to advise on a building.

In general, though, the British legacy is more modest than one would have thought, largely through the pride of the Chinese in their own traditions and the tendency of the colonial government to leave well alone.

Education is the area of greatest influence, since most of the early schools were started by missionaries and Churches. Later the government provided free schooling for all, although as late as the 1970s it lasted only until the age of thirteen. Unlike many of today's Western children, Chinese children bring to education a positive attitude, knowing that good marks and hard work will be likely to provide a comfortable and successful future. The consequence is that the Western values put out by the school system and the government are often taken on board in a very Chinese manner. The antismoking campaign is a case in point. Schools and government advertising told the public not to smoke, for their own good. People gave up smoking in enormous numbers, so compared to the mainland Hong Kong is fairly smoke-free.

More abstract values, such as honesty and justice, although undoubtedly present from Chinese culture, have been given a Western expression and prominence. A sense of "the rule of law" has been picked up, mostly from the British, simply from the good experience gained from its being in force for 150 years. It is high on the list of things that set Hong Kong apart from the mainland, and is guarded jealously by those who have seen how important it is in a fair society. This links with a disapproval of corruption that has made Hong Kong, with the help of the Independent Commission Against Corruption (see Colonial Governors, in Chapter 1), probably the least corrupt country in Asia.

Attitudes to social justice have slipped into Hong Kong mainly by way of the missionaries and the education they provided. The Christianity promulgated by early British and Americans in Hong Kong had a strong social ethic, and schools and charities were set up by them and later by their admirers. Nineteenth-century institutions such as the Po Leung Kuk, a charity for rescuing young servant girls, were set up by Hong Kong Chinese along the lines of Western charitable establishments—even their buildings having a grave Victorian air. Trade unions and discussions of equality and rights are also Western imports, but they are still less developed than in most Western countries. Environmental issues, again a Western initiative, are largely ignored by the general public, but campaigners such as Christine Loh are attempting to change this.

Inevitably, Hong Kong has a greater internationalism than the mainland. From its founding as a city, it was a trading post between the hugely differing cultures of Britain and China, and its attitudes are outward- rather than inward-looking. Businesspeople routinely travel around Asia and to the rest of the world, thinking no more of visiting Japan or Thailand for a couple of days than Americans might think of visiting a neighboring state. The universal concerns and discourse of international business are the common currency of their lives. More and more people go overseas for vacations, too, and they are becoming sophisticated travelers. However, they are famous for preferring Chinese food whenever they can, wherever they are!

Since Chinese traditions and old-fashioned Western ones overlap in so many areas, it is safe to say that if visitors behave in a sober and restrained manner, this will be fine with the Hongkongers. And if they fail to be offended by the unintended rudeness of the Chinese way, they will enjoy life in Hong Kong more.

MEN AND WOMEN

In the workplace, Hong Kong is one of the most equal societies. There are three women to every four men in employment, and although there are proportionately more women in lower-paid jobs, top management, the professions, and the civil service boast a high proportion. Discrimination on the basis of gender is not evident except possibly in restaurants, where men seem to catch waiters' eyes more successfully—but this can be true in the West too. However, in the home there is a lamentable shortage of "new men." Women who work a full day outside the home are generally expected to cook, clean, and care for children inside it as well.

Domestic Helpers

Many middle-class women are liberated from the chores at home and enabled to do paid work by the existence of a huge number of immigrant "domestic helpers," mainly from the Philippines but also from south Asia and Thailand. Chinese families often wish to employ Filipinas, with their comparatively good knowledge of English, to look after their children and teach them the rudiments of the language. These workers were the first people in Hong Kong to have a minimum wage. They send most of their money back to their families, and they have fixed-term contracts, renewable every two years. Their traditional day off is Sunday, when they tend to dress up and congregate in the public spaces and shopping malls in cheerful, voluble groups, swapping music CDs and drinking sodas. Occasionally you will see a Filipino, usually employed as a gardener or a musician, surrounded by a crowd of female compatriots.

Sexual Lifestyles

The Chinese have been reluctant to acknowledge homosexuality. It was illegal in Hong Kong until about twenty years ago, and still carries a stigma. Gay visitors are recommended to exercise cultural sensitivity and prudence in public places if they want to cause the least friction. However, there is a significant gay community, and the two gay clubs in Hong Kong are well frequented.

ATTITUDES TO WORK AND MONEY

Think of nineteenth-century industrialists in Britain and America, and you have something of the mentality of the Hong Kong Chinese to work and money. Work is not something to enjoy, but something that must be done. It is interesting that even for the industrious Chinese, once the money incentive has been taken away, work falls off. During the most stringent Communist rule in China, the workers had no incentives to work harder. Hong Kong Chinese dismissed them as lazy, and did not want them to come flooding in. Similarly, government service in Hong Kong was known as the "iron rice bowl" because it was so secure. Although most government workers were conscientious, a significant number of them put in the hours without working flat out. It is in business that the real work is done, because the rewards are directly linked.

Work is a commodity, and should take up most of your life and energy. It may be significant that the Cantonese for "go to work" actually means "go *back* to work," which implies that work is the normal and expected place to be. If you call an office early in the morning and the person you want is not there, you will be told, "He hasn't come back yet."

If you work hard enough, you will earn money, and money is the most important thing. Health and family are very important, but they are to some extent dependent on external factors, whereas money, in an economy like Hong Kong's, lies within the grasp of the individual.

Money is a good in itself; it is not particularly valued as a bringer of freedom or choice. More, it is the way of showing the status and importance of the family to whom it is accruing. Therefore it is the duty of everyone in the family to make as  much money as they can. It can be spent on education—when it is seen as an investment for the future—or on things that define status, such as precious objects, cars, fine clothes, and jewelry. In traditional Chinese society, a second or third wife or concubine was a public indication of wealth.

It is strongly believed that money should work for the family—it should be plowed into investments and businesses. If there is an abundance, it can be given to charity, and this will also increase the family's status, since the source of the donation will be publicly known. A hospital ward, or a school hall, for example, will probably, and preferably, bear the name of its donor.

The only anomalous use of money, to Western perception, is for gambling. True, the possible prizes may be very large, but the odds are usually so poor that it would seem a foolish enterprise to look on it as an investment. However, enormous amounts are spent on gambling each year by rich and poor alike, so the myth of luck prevails.

chapter three

CUSTOMS & TRADITIONS

RELIGION

Chinese Temples

As in most modern capitalist cities, religion is not a large part of most people's lives. The temples are nominally Buddhist, but various other gods and goddesses are enshrined in them. There is also a strong Taoist element. Before Buddhism spread throughout China in the sixth century CE, each region had its favorite local gods and goddesses. Since there is no notion of a right and a wrong way to pray to the higher powers, these local deities can be found along with Buddha and various other Chinese gods in many of the temples.

In Hong Kong, the goddess Tin Hau is a special favorite. She is the goddess of the sea, with a protective responsibility toward all mariners, and fishermen in particular. She is reputed to have been a fisherman's daughter who was kidnapped and taken in a ship far down the coast. A typhoon blew up, but she calmed the waters and saved the crew. You can find Tin Hau temples in the older fishing areas, notably Shek O, and on the outlying islands.

Another favorite is Kwan Yin, the goddess of mercy. She is entreated by anyone with a problem, and on days when the state lottery is drawn, many supplicants can be seen in her temples. There is a large statue of Kwan Yin in Repulse Bay, alongside the beach.

On the island of Cheung Chau, one of the oldest fishing communities, Pei Ti, god of water and the Spirit of the North, is most revered. He is also supplicated by fishermen, since he has the power to still storms and give good catches.

Unlike the rest of China, Hong Kong has not had any breaks in the religious observances of its people. After the Second World War, many Chinese from religious institutions in China settled in Hong Kong, and several are still there. Buddhist and Christian monasteries were established in the New Territories, particularly on Lantau Island. There is a large Buddhist community in the mountains there, and in 1995 the biggest Buddha in the world was erected on Lantau. It is a very popular place of pilgrimage—this is not a solemn occasion, but an excuse for an enjoyable day out in dramatic scenery. The monastery has a big temple and several gift shops, and offers a reasonably priced vegetarian lunch. Not that the average Hongkonger would eat only vegetables from choice. The special religious vegetarian meal is endured because it might confer merit, and even that includes chunky mushrooms and flavored bean curd that seem to imitate meat. Nominal Buddhists the Hongkongers may be, but vegetarian they are emphatically not, as many visiting veggies have found to their dismay.

Chinese temples are very worldly. Families wander around them, and apart from taking their shoes off before entering the inner temple no particular observances are necessary. Silence is not strictly observed. Animals come and go unhindered. Apart from the smoke from the joss sticks, there is no odor of sanctity, solemnity, or mysticism. Most worshipers will light a bunch of joss sticks and plant them into a sand-filled tub in front of their deity of choice, praying quietly as they do so. There is also a fortune-telling facility in larger temples. A cylindrical box full of long slivers of bamboo is used to obtain your fortune. On each sliver is a number. The petitioner shakes the box repeatedly, and after about half a minute, a sliver of bamboo inexplicably works its way up and out of the box. When it falls out, the petitioner picks it up and takes it to the priest for interpretation. The priest refers to a venerable book, in which each number has a prediction.

Fortune-Telling

When my son was one year old, I went to a temple on the outlying island of Po Toi, south of Hong Kong Island, to hear my fortune. There were no tourists there—just a few older people with serious intent. Leaving the baby with my husband, I shook my can of bamboo sticks. One fell out, and I took it to the old—and non-English-speaking—priest. Helpful locals with a smattering of English translated as he read out, "This is a person asking about a son. This son is like a fertile rice-field (he showed me the character for field, which I recognized), bringing a fair amount of money into the family." Twenty-five years later, I am proud to announce that this has come true!

Religion, Philosophy, or Superstition?

Even if organized religion is not a great part of people's lives, the general philosophy of life evolved in China, with Buddhist, Taoist, and Confucian elements, underpins traditional life to some extent. A holistic approach to the body and nature underlies most people's beliefs. In traditional medicine, exercise, and eating, the concept of *chi*, or energy flow (see Tai Chi, below), prevails.

It is also a truism that Hongkongers don't have a religion, they just have luck. Certainly there are a lot of quasi-religious practices that may be termed superstitions, particularly surrounding business and money. As you walk through the Hong Kong streets, you will often see huge flower- and ribbon-decked decorations arranged in front of a doorway. On closer inspection, you will see that a business is opening in that building today, and that the red or pink ribbons are inscribed with lucky wishes for the new restaurant or shop.

The business owner will have gone through many propitious deeds before the moment of opening. The *feng shui* (see below) of the building and of the space within it will have to be approved by a consultant. Furniture and ornaments will be chosen and placed with their recommendations in mind. Astrological predictions for the prosperity of the

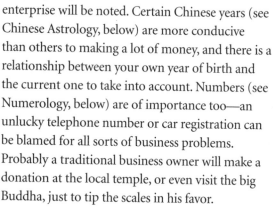

enterprise will be noted. Certain Chinese years (see Chinese Astrology, below) are more conducive than others to making a lot of money, and there is a relationship between your own year of birth and the current one to take into account. Numbers (see Numerology, below) are of importance too—an unlucky telephone number or car registration can be blamed for all sorts of business problems. Probably a traditional business owner will make a donation at the local temple, or even visit the big Buddha, just to tip the scales in his favor.

Other Religions

There are several flourishing Christian Churches and foundations in Hong Kong. Because of previous intolerance of Christianity in mainland China, several missions and religious bodies relocated to Hong Kong after 1950, and many are still there today. In addition, Christian schools and hospitals were established, providing good education and medicine at relatively low  prices for the local population, and many of these schools are still regarded as the best in the territory.

About 10 percent of the population belong to one of the Christian Churches.

Anglicans and Episcopalians are served by the cathedral in Central Hong Kong, Christ Church in Kowloon, and several other churches. Catholics, whose numbers have been greatly swelled by the population of Filipina domestic workers, have their cathedral close to the Anglican one, and nearly fifty churches throughout the territory.

Baptists are so well represented that they have a whole university to themselves in Kowloon, as well as churches, schools, and a hospital. The Seventh-Day Adventists, too, have a college and two hospitals in addition to their churches. Latter Day Saints (Mormons) also have a strong following.

Islam is also represented in the territory, with five mosques. The Muslim community in Hong Kong numbers about 70,000, about 1 percent of the total population. More than half are Chinese and many others are from Pakistan, Indonesia, and Malaysia.

Since the handover, religious freedom has continued to flourish, and the introduction of a holiday to mark Buddha's birthday has been seen as an improvement in relations between the government and religious bodies. Missionaries of all faiths can operate with no interference, and all the religious charitable institutions are thriving too.

FENG SHUI

In Cantonese, *feng shui* is pronounced "fung sui," and it is literally translated as "wind, water." Its general tenet, that man should live in harmony with nature, has spread its influence in the West in the last few decades. In its most basic application, *feng shui* is used to determine where to build a house, workplace, or temple. The compass was invented in China not for navigation, but for *feng shui*.

Hong Kong is the best place to find out about this four-thousand-year-old philosophy. The mainland Chinese government outlawed the practice of *feng shui* after the Revolution, in their bid to prevent "opiates of the people" sapping the drive to work hard for a Communist state. There is still official disapproval of anything regarded as superstitious. But in Hong Kong it flourished, and continues to do so. There are said to be more than ten thousand *feng shui* experts in Hong Kong and many of them have amassed tidy fortunes and glittering reputations.

Through the ages *feng shui* has acquired many extra areas of influence, so that every aspect of living and working space is susceptible to its energy. A house with its back to a wooded hill (for shelter) with an open outlook to the south over water (for light and air) is regarded by most people—not just the Chinese—as more desirable than a house in a damp hollow with hills in front of it, exposed to cold winds at the back. A river or a pond will increase wealth—undoubtedly true for arable farms and for fish or duck rearing. Villages in the New Territories still have *feng shui* woods behind them, which will protect them from wind or landslides. Thus far the Western property developer would agree, but *feng shui* goes much further than this. It addresses not only a building's proximity to natural features and other buildings, but also the shape and material of the building, shapes of rooms, positioning of doors, windows, and furniture, and even where in a room flowers or trinkets should be put. And it is all to harness the power of luck.

In Hong Kong, *feng shui* is widely practiced, and *feng shui* masters are in great demand and extremely well paid. At first glance, you might see that an astonishing number of buildings may benefit from the basic requirements of "hill behind, water in front," as the steep slopes of the Peak on Hong Kong Island and the hills of Kowloon and the New Territories provide just that. However, it can also be seen that buildings are crowded into the flatter areas with a concentration that no other city can match. Of necessity, these buildings are not sited in auspicious places, so the original tenets of *feng shui* have been stretched and bent to accommodate the needs of the people to maximize their luck.

The World's Most Expensive Tree?

Not only hills and rivers provide *feng shui* protection. Trees are important too. When Swire Properties were planning a huge shopping complex at Pacific Place, over the Admiralty MTR station, they encountered problems with a 130-year-old banyan tree, solidly rooted in the middle of their proposed development. They promised that it would be preserved at all costs. Cost was right – the "concrete flower pot" that eventually had to be constructed around it cost around HK $24 million (about US $3 million)—not counting the time spent by staff on its upkeep!

Although Central, the modern business district, is regarded by *feng shui* experts as adequately protected, the original area of British commerce was not so lucky. It was in a flat and mosquito-infested marshy area, misnamed Happy Valley. There was a bad outbreak of malaria in the mid-nineteenth century, which the Chinese workers living there blamed on the inauspicious *feng shui*. Gradually, business moved to the luckier area a couple of miles down the road.

The area of Central where most banks and prestigious firms have their headquarters is reputedly situated on a dragon's vein, which brings a lot of luck and wealth. When the Hongkong and Shanghai Bank was built, great care was taken to make the most this lucky vein. The shape of the bank apparently suggests a laughing Buddha, and the governors of the bank ensured a clear view to the harbor (and the money it represents) by paying for a recreational square and underground parking in front of it. Escalators taking visitors to the main banking hall are strangely curved—again for *feng shui* reasons.

Uphill from the Hongkong Bank, and also on the rich vein, is the Bank of China, designed by I. M. Pei. The design is, however, not respected by *feng shui* experts. It is based on triangles, which are inauspicious in themselves. It is to the surroundings that the bank presents the most menace, however. In particular, it has a very sharp corner pointing directly toward Government House and the Central Government Offices. Such a corner is thought to be like a dagger pointing at the heart of the Hong Kong administration. Before the advent of the Bank of China, Government House was auspiciously located and oriented. Could it be that even in the early days of British rule, *feng shui* was taken into account?

Another corner of the Bank of China points toward the Legislative Council building, where parliament is based. As if that weren't bad enough, the two projecting masts, or "chopsticks," on top of the building point upward, resembling nothing so closely as the incense sticks used to honor the dead.

Color schemes, rearrangement of furniture, and other measures can be recommended to counter chronic bad luck. Moving house or offices is a last resort in hard times.

Westerners in Hong Kong have also succumbed to the "insurance" mentality of *feng shui* believers. You may as well get it right, just in case. When Marks & Spencer first came to the territory, it didn't do very well, but after the *feng shui* expert had recommended tactically placed lights, wooden turtles, and fish tanks, sales picked up. A branch of McDonald's in Kowloon is reputed to have a tank of piranha fish—quite a draw in itself, one might think, as a curiosity!

The Hong Kong Tourist Association offers *feng shui* tours of some of the most obvious landmarks of this ubiquitous practice.

Mirrors and Water

Luckily, a relatively cheap means of protecting yourself against neighboring buildings and other inauspicious things exists. All you have to do is hang a small, hexagonal mirror, called a *bat gwa* mirror, in such a way that it reflects the bad luck back to its source. The theory is that an evil being will be repelled by seeing itself in such a mirror. Making sure the sea or other water is reflected in a *bat gwa* mirror, on the other hand, can increase the financial fortunes of a company. Since water represents money (and *sui*, water, is the slang term for money), you may notice that most banks and businesses have water features somewhere about the buildings, or at least a fish tank in the lobby.

NUMEROLOGY

Numbers have always fascinated scholars in every culture, and Chinese numerology is complicated and subtle. It goes with *feng shui*.

Personal numerology is usually based on birth date, but numbers come into everyday life in many ways, and all the numbers in your life have significance.

The sort of numerology that visitors may come across in Hong Kong is centered in the sounds of the words in Cantonese:

Yi (two) sounds like the word for "easy."

Saam (three) sounds like the word for "alive," or "lifelong."

Sei (four) sounds like the word for "death."

Baat (eight) sounds like the word for "prosperity."

Sapsaam (thirteen) sounds like "sure life."

By extension, twenty-four sounds like "easy to die," and so is considered very unlucky; 28 sounds like "easy prosperity," so is very fortunate; 138 sounds like "prosperity all your life," and 168 like "everlasting prosperity"—and you can't get luckier than that.

The Luck in Numbers

A friend with a lot of fours in his telephone number was warned to change it. A particular office telephone number meant "Luck, lots of luck, all along the road luck." Car license plates with lucky numbers are sold for enormous sums.

CHINESE ASTROLOGY

Like its Western counterpart, Chinese astrology divides people into twelve basic types, although there are several subdivisions. Instead of being based on the month and date of the year in which you are born, the Chinese system looks at the year of birth. Each year is named after an animal, and begins at Chinese New Year—between one and two months after January 1. Each animal has its own characteristics, which are not always the ones you might expect.

The Twelve Animals

As with Western astrology, the origins of the twelve-animal system are lost in the mists of time. There is a charming legend, however.

The Jade King of Heaven was feeling a little bored, and decided he wanted to see some representatives of the animal kingdom on Earth. Envoys were sent to Earth to produce twelve assorted animals.

The first to be invited were the Cat and the Rat. The Rat didn't want the Cat to come, for obvious reasons, so tricked him out of his invitation. Ten others were invited too: the Ox, the Tiger, the Rabbit, the Dragon, the Snake, the Horse, the Goat (or Ram), the Monkey, the Cock (or Rooster), and the Dog. They duly appeared and presented themselves in front of the Jade King's palace; but the King noticed that there were only eleven. An envoy was sent down for another animal, and the first thing he saw was someone carrying a Pig, so that was added to the others.

The Rat, inclined to show off, hopped on to the back of the Ox, and played a tune on his flute. The Jade King, impressed, gave Rat the first place in the line, followed by the patient Ox. He liked the courage of the Tiger, and put it third, and then the rest in order: Rabbit, Dragon, Snake, Horse, Goat, Monkey, Cock, Dog, and Pig.

So every twelve years there is a new cycle, starting with the Rat, who is the cleverest in the zodiac. However, in Vietnam, they claim that the Cat took the year that the Chinese give to the Rabbit! But their characteristics are the same.

The characteristics of people born in different years are, roughly, as follows:

Rat: clever, charming, imaginative; can be conspiratorial.

Ox: straightforward, kind, patient; can be dull.

Tiger: courageous, loyal, honorable; can be critical.

Rabbit: diplomatic, peace-loving, intuitive; can be indecisive.

Dragon: magnetic, dynamic, lucky; can be intolerant.

Snake: elegant, self-contained, perceptive; can be obstinate.
Horse: enthusiastic, flexible, cheerful; can be impatient.
Goat: creative, sensitive, imaginative; can be irresponsible.
Monkey: independent, sociable, shrewd; can be manipulative.
Cock: flamboyant, obliging, resilient; can be vain.
Dog: humane, tolerant, idealistic; can be anxious.
Pig: easy-going, sympathetic, sensual; can be spendthrift.

Because the Lunar New Year starts on a different calendar date each year, it is difficult for people with January and February birthdays to calculate their animal year without a special table. For the others, it is enough to know that the Year of the Rat started in early 1900 and recurs every twelve years.

There are five elements in the Chinese system, and therefore each year has a secondary name: Earth, Fire, Water, Metal, and Wood. Each combination recurs only once in sixty years. The year 1966 was the year of the Fire Horse, and children born in this year are thought to be wild and uncontrollable. There were significantly fewer births in Hong Kong that year than in the other years in the decade.

Each year has its own character, and astrologers in Hong Kong are quick to point out the advantages and disadvantages of each year as it turns. For the record, there have been about 4,702 Chinese years to date.

TAI CHI AND *CHI GUNG*

You may, if you are an early riser or plagued by jet lag, find a surprising number of people out and about at 6:00 a.m. The parks and open areas will certainly be host to groups of people, many of them elderly, practicing the ancient art of *tai chi*. Originally, like most of the three hundred different styles of bodywork, *tai chi* was a martial art. It emphasizes stability of the body, and does not have the high-energy kicks of the *kung fu* movies. *Tai chi* (translated as "great ultimate") is characterized by being gentle and yielding. You can become mesmerized watching the slow, focused movements. They have the qualities of a flowing river, yielding to the solid and fixed, sweeping away the weak and unstable.

Chi, or *qi*, is the energy flow within all living things, sometimes defined as "that which distinguishes the living from the dead." If this flow is blocked, weak, or out of balance, you will become ill—physically, mentally, or spiritually. The term *chi gung* (*qigong*) means "*chi* work" and is used as a blanket term for all exercises that work on the *chi*. It works from the outside of the body inward—so that when you have done the regime of physical exercises, you should be feeling healthier internally, both in body and spirit. It is "a path and not a destination," so is practiced as a daily ritual to ensure a healthy, balanced life. It may be said that the Chinese believe in *chi* as a kind of universal life force, and that this force has been externalized in other cultures and named "God."

The Origin of Tai Chi

Tai chi is alleged to have been founded by a Taoist mystic and hermit, Chang San-feng, who probably lived in the thirteenth century in central China. The legend has it that Master Chang was out walking in the forest when he saw a snake engaged in a fight with a crane. Chang was impressed at the ingenious way the snake was able to feint, elude, and counterattack the large, powerful bird. That night, the art of *tai chi* came to him in a dream.

FESTIVALS AND HOLIDAYS

Hong Kong people work hard, but their calendar is liberally sprinkled with holidays, both Chinese and Western. There are twelve statutory paid holidays a year* to which employees are entitled, and there are several additional causes for celebration throughout the year.

January 1	New Year's Day*
Jan/Feb	Three days at Lunar (or Chinese) New Year*
Mar/Apr	Ching Ming*
	Three days at Easter
May 1	Labor Day*
May 26	The Buddha's Birthday*
June 15	Tuen Ng, or Dragonboat Festival*
July 1	Hong Kong SAR Establishment Day*
October 1	Chinese National Day
September	Day following the Mid-Autumn Festival*
October	Chung Yeung*
December	Chinese Winter Solstice Festival (Dong Zhi), or Christmas Day in lieu*

Chinese New Year

By far the most important festival is the Lunar or Chinese New Year, which marks the beginning of spring. Beware of planning anything at this time—most people do not work over the three days, and banks and businesses will be firmly shut. Chinese New Year falls on a different date each year, but it corresponds to the new moon between mid-January and mid-February, and lasts three days.

As in Scotland, the first person you meet must bring you luck. In Hong Kong's case, a red-clad person would be especially lucky. Red or colored songbirds are also a good omen.

The first and second days of the celebrations are a time for family reunions, and the streets are quiet on these days. Traditionally, a religious thanksgiving for Heaven, Earth, and the family accompanies the gatherings. The most important focus of this is the union of the ancestors with the living members of the family. Ancestors are deeply respected, because they laid the foundations of each family, and are felt to be still with the family in spirit. They are honored with a special New Year's Eve dinner. On the third day of New Year, people can leave their families and go out and have fun.

The New Year symbolizes sweeping away the old and adopting the new. Debts must be paid and houses cleaned by the end of the old year, so that a new start can be made. On the stroke of midnight on New Year's Eve, every door and window in the house must be open to allow the old year out. Firecrackers and other fireworks welcome the new one in.

There is a feeling that anything that happens on the first day of the year will continue for the whole year. So positive language and laughter are encouraged, and arguing, crying, and dwelling on the past are avoided. Children and younger relatives as well as unmarried friends are given *laisee*, little red envelopes with crisp new banknotes inside, for good fortune. Patriarchs of families and important people in the community will have dozens of these red packets at their disposal so that they can dispense good fortune far and wide.

Probably more food is consumed during the New Year celebrations than at any other time of the year. On New Year's Day, Chinese families eat a vegetarian dish called *jai*. Other foods include a whole fish, to represent togetherness and abundance, and a whole chicken for prosperity. Noodles should not be cut, as they represent long life. Desserts made of sweet, glutinous rice are very popular in Cantonese cuisine.

Ching Ming and Chung Yeung

Also known as the Grave-sweeping Festival, or Spring Remembrance, Ching Ming takes place at the third moon. Chinese families visit the graves of their ancestors to clear away weeds, tidy the area, light incense, and make offerings of wine and fruit. The day is celebratory in feel—more like a picnic than a solemn memorial.

Chung Yeung, which occurs six months later, is Autumn Remembrance, so much the same sort of thing happens. It is also traditionally good to go up into the hills at Chung Yeung, because there is a legend about a man who was advised to take his family to a high place for the ninth day of the ninth month. When they returned, they found that their village had been destroyed by enemies.

Buddha's Birthday
Worshipers show their devotion by washing Buddha's statues. Vegetarian meals are eaten. Celebrations center on the major temples and monasteries in Hong Kong.

Cheung Chau Bun Festival
This is special to Hong Kong. It takes place at the full moon of the fourth month, usually in May. The villagers of Cheung Chau, an island with an ancient fishing community, erect huge bamboo towers near the Pak Tai Temple. On the towers are fixed sweet buns together with effigies of three gods. For three days the islanders become vegetarian. On the final day a colorful procession winds through the village streets. Children, elaborately costumed and made up, are supported on tiny seats held up by adults. They look as though they are standing on top of poles. They make their way to the temple where, for safety reasons, the old practice of climbing the

towers to seize the buns has been discontinued. The buns are distributed in a more orderly fashion after a religious ceremony.

Tuen Ng Festival

This has now become known internationally as the Dragon Boat Festival, although the races were inaugurated only in 1976. Over a hundred teams from across the globe participate in the waters around Hong Kong. After the locals have raced, the event becomes an international open. The main competitions take place on Shing Mun River, at Sha Tin in the New Territories. Teams of twenty-two or twenty-four paddle their long, elaborately carved, colorful boats to the beat of heavy drums. The boats have dragon's heads and tails.

The festival commemorates the death of a popular national hero, Qu Yuan, who drowned himself during the third century BC, in protest against a corrupt government. As locals tried to rescue him, they beat drums to scare fish away and threw dumplings into the sea to keep the fish from eating his body. During the festival, people eat rice-and-meat dumplings wrapped in bamboo leaves.

Mid-Autumn Festival

Another excuse for a family reunion occurs on the fifteenth day of the eighth month of the lunar calendar. This is the Mid-Autumn Festival, Moon Festival, or Lantern Festival. The full moon's shape symbolizes the family circle. The special food associated with this festival is a moon cake, a sweet, heavy cake with a filling of sugar, fat, sesame, lotus seeds, walnut, and a golden egg yolk, which is reminiscent of the moon. To eat their moon cakes, families gather on hillsides, carrying colorful paper lanterns in various animal or vehicle shapes, and view the moon.

Prohibitions

Hong Kong has plenty of warning signs everywhere, and there is no excuse for ignoring them. There are quite a number of different prohibitions, although the sign of a pig with a red line across it ("No animals") that used to decorate the MTR in the early days has, alas, gone.

Many public places and offices as well as the MTR ban smoking, so ask before you light up.

Cell phones are also becoming less tolerated in Western-style restaurants, so pay attention to signs.

LITTLE POINTS OF ETIQUETTE

• Toothpicks are like networking—used at every meal. Put your left hand discreetly over the one holding the toothpick, in the manner of someone shading eyes from glare.

• Don't show the soles of your feet to others. Putting your feet on a chair, or on a train seat, is regarded as very bad manners.

• Even left-handers use chopsticks in their right hand. Sit at a crowded round table with everyone eating, and you'll see why!

• Don't leave chopsticks vertically in your bowl. They'd look like incense sticks in a bowl of ashes—a sure reminder of death.

• Give and receive business cards, and other pieces of paper, with both hands. One hand looks casual to the point of rudeness.

• Flip-flops or thonged sandals are not allowed in certain hotel lobbies and restaurants. Other sandals are tolerated.

• If you are invited to a wedding, it is appropriate to give money, not objects.

- It is considered polite to refuse an invitation or gift once, and then to demur and accept it gracefully.

- Displays of affection, temper, or anything "extreme" are frowned upon.

- White is the color of death, and black and white on a flowered display panel commemorate a death. Blue also has some intimations of mortality. Red is the favored color for celebration, happiness, starting a business, announcing a wedding, and almost everything else. In colonial government circles, however, only the governor himself was allowed to use red ink! Yellow is the color of luck and good fortune, and was the imperial color.

chapter four

AT HOME

THE FAMILY

Traditionally, the Chinese were divided into clans, each with a particular surname and an ancestral village. Daughters would marry men from other clans and move away to other villages. Sons would bring wives in from other villages. For this reason, daughters were not prized. They were often called "holes in the rice bag"—they ate, but in the end they just left the family, and had to be given money to marry. That is one of the most powerful reasons behind the traditional prejudice against female children. Although this has changed a great deal with the advent of women's equality, particularly in the marketplace, there is still a certain prejudice in favor of male children, generally among the older and less well-educated.

Demographically, Hong Kong is a developed industrial territory, having birth and death rates as low as Germany or Japan. The population continues to grow because of migration from other parts of China. Young men and women from mainland China are eager to work there, sometimes as a first step to further foreign travel.

Many couples have no children, and many have only one child. Factors responsible for this include cramped living conditions, full employment, and compulsory education. The population has moved from the old-style huge families with a high infant mortality rate to this modern lifestyle in just two generations. With the change has come a loosening of ties to the older generation.

The average age in Hong Kong is thirty-seven, older than that of neighboring countries, and the average life expectancy around eighty years. Many old people do not have grandchildren, and are not wanted in their busy children's small flats. As a result, there is a thin but steady stream of retired people crossing to the mainland, to the ancestral villages they may have left as children. There has been little mobility in China, and the chances are that there will still be some family members in the villages. Newcomers will be especially welcome if they bring the accoutrements of the Hong Kong lifestyle, including the latest Japanese audiovisual equipment and imported cosmetics.

LIFESTYLES

Hong Kong has changed over the past thirty years from a city of poor incomers from China with a largely British civil service and a few rich merchants of all nationalities to a relatively middle-class city, with a larger number of well-off people. Along with this rise in wealth has come a great change in lifestyle.

The main transformation has come in housing. In 1970, more than a million people lived in "squatter huts"—roughly made shacks with no ownership title, no services or amenities, and no modern conveniences. Enterprising individuals ran water pipes up the steep hillsides and connected dangerously swinging electric cables to flimsy sockets, all illegal and unpaid for, but tolerated because of the huge pressure of population.

Now, apart from some old squatter areas that have been "saved" (and upgraded) due to popular demand, most of the population live in high-rise apartment blocks and have enough money to acquire the latest music and entertainment systems as well as modern kitchens and bathrooms. But space is still at a premium. It's not uncommon to find five or six people living in an apartment that in the West would hold one or two. Ikea, the Swedish furnishing company, and its local imitators, have prospered mightily by providing cleverly designed and versatile furniture for very small apartments. A favorite unit consists of a bunk-bed on top with a workstation underneath, incorporating drawers and lighting—just right for the ambitious young schoolchild.

The cramped and crowded nature of Hong Kong life has resulted in a particular kind of lifestyle. Within the family sharing an apartment, it may be quite normal for people not to talk intimately or involve the others in their lives outside. Because there is so much physical closeness, individuals ensure the privacy that enables them to keep sane by a certain mental or emotional distance.

Emotional Space

A work colleague lived with her brother and his wife, and her elderly father. Their relationships were cordial but distant. She did not know where her brother or her sister-in-law worked, whether they were going away for Chinese New Year, or where they had been on vacation abroad. No friend or colleague had ever been invited to her apartment, which was very near her office.

Because of this, nearly all socializing takes place outside the home. It is normal to eat out for every meal, even breakfast, and these meals are rarely taken alone. This makes life much more interesting for the visitor—all human life is out there, on the streets, in the malls, in the parks, and in all the shops and restaurants.

It is said that a Hongkonger on his or her own will sing rather than bear the silence. Those having to be by themselves—for instance traveling to work—will almost certainly be listening to a walkman or talking on a cell phone. Nature abhors a vacuum, and Hong Kong abhors a silence. This constant noise, which rises to a crescendo in the packed restaurants at lunchtime, can bother foreign visitors from more tranquil places. But tune it out, and you will enjoy your time amid the bustling crowds a lot more.

The open areas are popular at all times of year. Snacks are eaten on park benches and outside the small, absurdly cheap eating places known as *daai pai dong*—nowadays hard to find in the central districts, but still flourishing in outer suburbs and new towns. In fast-food and cheaper restaurants you will probably find fierce air-conditioning to counter the body warmth of the patrons and the high temperature of the traditional stir fries.

The average Hongkonger keeps fit by walking, whether it's walking to work, using the narrow pedestrian bridges that span the city streets in an elaborate network, indulging in the favorite pastime—window shopping—or using the weekends to visit outlying islands and New Territories nature trails with family, friends, and accompanying music. In the summer, the beaches are packed, lifeguards perched in watchtowers along the shoreline.

Fashion is conservative. Most younger women wear Western styles, but not to the extreme. Some of the older men and women still wear traditional Chinese clothes— a pajama suit with a high collar.

Taboos

Like other Far Easterners, the Hong Kong Chinese are not a tactile people. Hugging might offend; shaking hands is acceptable but not essential. The most taboo bodily matter to be aware of is not to show the soles of ones feet to anyone.

Gambling

Gambling could reasonably be said to be the Hongkongers' favorite vice. Going to the racing at Happy Valley and Shatin are extremely popular, and the races are watched by millions on TV.

At home, a very popular game played for money, equivalent to cards, is *mah-jong*. It is played with a number of small tiles that are collected and discarded at great speed, causing the cheerful noise of plastic on wood heard all over the territory, in particular during a stroll through the fishing villages of the outer islands, where there is no traffic to shatter the peace.

This love of gambling has been harnessed to provide useful government revenue. As early as the 1860s, Tung Wah, a major Hong Kong Chinese charitable organization, was founded, with hospitals and welfare centers.

There is a national lottery called the Mark Six, somewhat similar to state lotteries in other countries. Six numbers are chosen from a total of forty-nine. Since it was started in 1975, the Mark Six has contributed over HK $22 billion to the Government Treasury and the Lotteries Fund, a charitable fund supporting various causes.

NAMES

The tradition in China is that there are "a hundred surnames." There may be a few more, but basically you will encounter the same names over and over again. Each surname refers to a huge extended family, or clan, and was originally associated with a particular town or village, whose members would all have had the same surname.

The surname precedes the given names. Li Ka-shing is Mr. Li, not Mr. Ka-shing. Immigrants to English-speaking countries were often mistakenly called by their given names, and didn't think to complain, so for example, Chan Ting's family in New Zealand have now become the Ting family, and the Chan is lost forever. It is usual for someone to be referred to by his or her surname only. Using a title is normal and polite, but the next step to informality would be to use just the surname. Chinese given names are rarely used in speech. They, and family nicknames, are felt to be private, and it would be wrong for a foreign visitor to start using a given name or nickname in the hope of showing a more informal relationship.

Surnames do not always have a resonance of meaning, but the derivation is often buried in the character. Cheung is a form of the word meaning "long," and Li or Lee "plum tree."

Most given names consist of two words, conventionally written in various ways according to taste: Ka-shing as above is generally hyphenated in Hong Kong, but mainland names are written in Pinyin (a different form of romanization), in which given names appear as one word, for example Mao Zedong rather than Mao Tse-tung.

The meaning of given names is generally known and important. Women now often have names like Yuk-bing (jade ice) or Mei-ling (very beautiful), but previously there was not much gender differentiation. Most names tend to focus on the good qualities you might wish to attract to your child, such as Ming (bright), or Yan (kindness).

For use in Western-style businesses, many Hong Kong Chinese choose Western names, or approximations of them. These often sound like their original names—Winnie for Wing-man, and Mabel for Mei-yan, for example. Fashions nowadays follow American or English ones, with Karen, Kelly, Candy, and Darren existing alongside Billy and Winnie. There may not be much research into the meaning or spelling of a name, but they have some connection with the Chinese name. Scholar, Bright, Radiant, Lovely, Happy, and Silent (a girl) obviously hope to attract the right character and may be direct translations of the Chinese names. Superman, Jesus, Janus, and Hermes invoke suitable role models. You may find Paulson, Dickson, and Lawson have fathers called Paul, Richard, and Lawrence. Then there are names that sound vaguely like the Chinese: Juicy (Juicy Tang has been spotted at a supermarket checkout), Mantis, Heman (a girl), Fatman, Elvin, Pacman, and Iceman. Yet others have fantasy names, usually taken from advertisements: Benz, Bentley, Hoover, Coffee, Apple.

EDUCATION

Education is taken very seriously by Hongkongers. As a largely first- or second-generation immigrant community with very few resources to back them up, they perceive their children's brains to be their fortune. So schooling is long and hard, and academic achievement admired—not for its own sake, but for the earning power it gives.

Educational content and examinations are directed by government and continue to have the British shape and style of the 1970s, although in Britain itself considerable changes have occurred since then. Education is provided free for all from the age of six to sixteen.

Early Education

Nursery schools and kindergartens take children as young as eighteen months, and they soon start the business of learning. Rhymes and elementary arithmetic start young. Chinese children seem to have an innate  ability to concentrate at an early age, and it is common to see a class of three-year-olds all looking at the teacher and not fidgeting. Modern methods have introduced much more play and activity into the classroom at this stage but traditionally, this was a time for rote-learning.

Primary school starts at the age of six. Most schools have two shifts, so the school day may be from 7:30 a.m. to 1:30 p.m., or 1:00 p.m. to 5:00 p.m. Classes tend to be large. Learning to read and write Chinese takes years, as each character must be learned from scratch, and some require as many as twenty-two separate strokes of the pen. From the beginning, homework is given, and it is not unusual to hear of children at primary school working three hours a day outside class time. There is little space for play areas, so education is very sedentary even for small children.

Secondary Education
By this time, the children are accustomed to hard work and lots of homework. Even though taught in classes of forty to fifty, they outstrip most other cultures in exam achievement, and attribute this to the sheer amount of work put in, on the assumption that practice makes perfect. One girl who later went to boarding school in England said, "Here they think four math problems for homework is a lot. I am used to doing fourteen."

Most children attend the government schools, but there are some important and prestigious private schools run by Christian and other charitable organizations. The fees are not high, but the intake is selective and preference is given to sons and daughters of alumni. In this way an elite has arisen in the past fifty years, and many top professionals and businesspeople come from it.

There are several international schools. The English Schools Foundation provides an English-medium education with the English curriculum and exam system. Although these schools were started for British children, at least two-thirds of their intake are from other countries, notably India and other Asian countries. There are currently children of fifty-five different nationalities in this system. Nationality may be misleading, as many students with British, Canadian, or Australian passports are in fact ethnic Chinese, their parents having emigrated to establish foreign nationality and then returned to resume making money in their home territory.

Higher Education

Such is the demand for education that there are six universities in Hong Kong. The oldest and perhaps the most prestigious is the University of Hong Kong, officially established in 1911. It occupies some gracious old buildings and a welter of new blocks to the west of Hong Kong Island.

There are also a number of specialist colleges, such as the HK Academy for Performing Arts, and private schools of commerce and language.

SOCIALIZING

EATING OUT

Eating out is very popular, and is
the favorite way to socialize.
"The more the merrier" is the
general rule, and there will
often be ten to fourteen
people sitting around a table
for an office lunch or family
meal. The tables in Chinese restaurants are geared
to this size of party. It is customary to order as
many dishes as there are participants, which gives a
lot of variety, and a "lazy Susan" in the middle of
the big round table ensures that everyone can reach
the food and help themselves to every dish. *Dim
sum* may be ordered at lunchtime (see Cantonese
Food, in Chapter 7, and The Banquet, on p.110).

Smaller social lunches or other meals may take
place not in a Chinese restaurant but in one of the
myriad others. Thai and Italian food are both very
popular, and the tables are of a normal Western
size, so two to six diners can eat more intimately
and comfortably together.

TIPPING

The smarter hotels and restaurants add a 10 to 15 percent service charge to the bill, but it is usual to leave an additional tip of a few HK dollars to the room staff or waiter, and this will probably go to the individual rather than into a common fund. In ordinary restaurants where no service charge is added, most people leave five or ten HK dollars, or add between 5 and 10 percent to the bill. Western-style coffee shops don't add a service charge, but there is usually a "tips box."

Most taxi drivers don't expect a tip, but it is usual to round the fare up to the nearest HK dollar, or the nearest five dollars on a longer journey. There are standard extra charges for baggage and late-night trips.

In general, if you have received better-than-average service, give a tip—it will be welcomed.

ENTERTAINING
At Home

It is not common for Hong Kong Chinese to entertain at home. However, it may happen. Guests should arrive on time, and leave relatively early. A suitable gift for the host would be a bottle of good Scotch or brandy, with some candy or cookies.

These should all be decoratively wrapped. Don't expect your host to open what you bring—this is regarded as greedy and impatient. Likewise, if someone gives you a present, do not open it immediately, or in their presence. Put it on one side to open later, and thank the person next time you see them.

Often a modest host and hostess will deprecate what they have, and apologize for the food. Your job as a good guest is to praise the food, so an equilibrium is reached. Beware of praising an *objet d'art* excessively in someone's home, in case the host feels an obligation to give it to you!

Business Entertaining

If you meet people from a large company, they may have other means of entertaining you at their disposal. One big perk is the junk, which is no longer a picturesque sailing vessel but a motorboat with a wooden superstructure holding up to forty people. The junk trip used to be mainly an expatriate diversion, but has grown in popularity with other groups. Trips are made on weekends to outlying islands, where drinks and lunch are served at anchor. Swimming and sometimes other water sports are available. You may also be invited in the evening to take a junk trip to an island famous for its seafood restaurants. It's a very pleasant way of getting out of the city, and on a warm evening you will have a beautiful view of the city lights.

Another organized outing might be to the races. Horse racing is something of an institution in Hong Kong. Everyone seems to go, although children are not allowed. The tracks are flat, and the races short, but the amount of money gambled on one race can be phenomenal. Hong Kong ranks third in the world in total betting (about $10 billion a year), after Japan and the United States. Bear in mind that Japan's betting covers nearly 24,000 races a year, and America's 55,000. Hong Kong has about 700 races all told.

The lower reaches of the stadia (there are two, one in Happy Valley and one in Sha Tin) house a pushing, noisy crowd and several flourishing food and drink stalls. The upper reaches, where a business bigwig might have a "box," are very different. Each box is in fact a suite of rooms with a private viewing terrace, and superb catering is usually provided. If you are enjoying your meal so much that you do not want to get up to go to the viewing terrace, you only have to turn your head to see one of the special televisions installed for those in the boxes. If you step outside the box, you can place bets with calm, uniformed women reminiscent of bank tellers. A poker face is necessary in Chinese society. Whether you win or lose, it is prudent to remain passive.

Another outing might involve a cultural show, for example Cantonese opera, although this is an acquired taste and lasts for four hours or more, so many Chinese businesspeople would not expect Westerners to appreciate it.

THE BANQUET

The word "banquet" is barely used in Western entertainment, but it means something quite specific to the Chinese. It is a formal Chinese dinner, sometimes for one  table but very often for several, hosted by one person or a company. The menu is planned in advance, and copies of it will appear on each table so the guests can pace themselves. Normally, twelve or fourteen courses are served, following a certain order, although individual dishes may vary. Nearly every dish contains protein, so at one banquet you may have as many as twelve different types of meat, poultry, and fish. The dish is served into individual bowls, and the bowls are handed to each guest. When each course is ready to be eaten, it is usual to drink a toast to it. Watch everyone else and try to imitate them. Hold your glass up in your right hand and support it at the bottom with the left, and make a circular gesture around the table, making eye contact where possible. Then take a sip—whether it be tea, soda, beer, or brandy. Then pick up your chopsticks when your host does, and enjoy the food.

First comes a dish of cold cuts, sometimes with a few salad vegetables. After this, dishes such as whole steamed garoupa (grouper) and bird's nest soup will appear, one by one. Sometimes an honored guest will be given a choice morsel by the host, and needless to say it should be received with thanks and eaten with pleasure. This can be difficult if the dish is one that is unfamiliar, such as chicken's feet with pork fat, but an attempt should be made to eat some of it. It is expected that you will leave something in your bowl, so that you do not look greedy for more.

A banquet shows how wealthy the host is, so rice and noodles are served only at the very end, in case anyone is still hungry. It is quite polite not to eat either of these; in fact it would be impolite to finish your bowl, as it would imply you have not been well fed and want more.

The very last course may be a sweet dessert, but is often an orange, which is served whole with the peel on. It is the signal for the end of the banquet, and hosts will get up after they've had their oranges. When your hosts go, you must too, even if you haven't had time to eat the orange. The hosts will stand at the exit to the room and guests thank them, by putting their hands together and bowing slightly, or by shaking the right hand of the host with both hands and bowing.

Using chopsticks is an art that it is worthwhile to acquire. Hold the top chopstick about half to two-thirds down, like a pencil. Then fit the second stick in between the third and fourth fingers and manipulate this in a pincer movement to pick up the food. This is comparatively easy with pieces of meat or a leafy vegetable, but peanuts and similarly smooth, round objects present quite a challenge. Note that if you are not being served by a waiter, taking food from the center of the table with your chopsticks and putting it directly into your mouth is regarded as impolite. It should be put into your bowl first, usually with a spoon.

At elaborate or charity banquets, small but expensive gifts are put in each place, and at company banquets there are very often lucky draws for presents—you may have been given a ticket with a winning number. This all gives face to the hosts, who are seen as generous, and you are then in their debt to some extent.

Karaoke
Business entertaining often includes karaoke after a banquet. It is a great favorite in Hong Kong. Before

the days of karaoke, only the most intrepid or inebriated guests would take the floor and sing unaccompanied, but now nobody has an excuse not to sing along. Some foreigners feel they just cannot join in with this form of entertainment, but others love it. Your standing will rise considerably if you take the plunge! If the banquet has gone well, then the lubricants will have taken over and most barriers broken down. It's important that locals start the singing, as foreigners will often follow—even for just one effort. A bonus is to get the foreigner singing a duet with his/her counterpart. As a rule, have a go.

For the serious *aficionados* of karaoke, there are numerous karaoke bars in Hong Kong, ranging from the seedy to the opulent.

Suzie Wong

Foreign visitors are often fascinated by the world of Suzie Wong—the readily available and submissive young Asian beauty— and think the Orient should provide a mystique interlinked with sexual entertainment. However, the Vietnam days of "R & R" have been replaced by the age of AIDS awareness. Your business colleagues will not send any "live entertainment" to your hotel room unless you have expressed a wish for it, though you should be on the lookout for a subtle hint from a local who is trying to gauge your wishes.

chapter six

TIME OUT

GETTING AROUND

Traveling around Hong Kong can be a delight.
There is probably a greater variety of forms of
transportation than in any other city in the world.

Paying for all kinds of public transportation is
best done by means of an Octopus Card. This is a
smart card that can be used on all major forms of
transportation as well as in various food outlets
and phone booths. It will work through a bag or
wallet, and so can be used with a minimum of
inconvenience. The smart chip can even be put
into a ring or other fashion item—this is very
popular with the locals. Tourist deals on Octopus
Cards are not especially good value, especially if
you buy a separate airport-to-city ticket for that
express journey. Otherwise, make sure you have
plenty of small change, as payment is often made
by putting coins into a box on boarding or leaving.

Sea

Because of the fragmented nature of the terrain,
ferries are used quite a bit. The Star Ferry that plies

between Hong Kong Island and the Kowloon peninsula is a famous sight, unchanged for well over a century. Each ship has a name ending in Star, and has a comforting, rounded shape and distinctive green paintwork. The fares are low, and the comfort minimal, but it is one of the best ways of looking at the harbor. The seats have backs that can be swung across so that you can sit facing either direction, which is a simple and effective way of maximizing the views.

The outlying islands are accessed by two types of ferry, the slow, ordinary ones, and smoother, more modern craft, and the trip alone is worth it. You swoop out of the harbor past the city and see unfolding vistas of peninsulas and islands—most clad in buildings but as you get further from the center, just dark green with dense scrub.

Rail

There is a good underground network, the MTR (Mass Transit Railway), the LRT (Light Rail Transit) that links towns in the eastern New Territories, and the KCR (Kowloon-Canton Railway), a regular rail link to the northern New Territories and China. All these are very busy at peak times, and you can miss your stop on the MTR if you are wedged in the middle of a car. Much of the rest of the time it is the best way to travel for a distance of more than about a mile, being air-conditioned, smoke-free, frequent, fast, and very clean.

To ascend the Peak for the first time, the Peak Tram is the only way, unless you are of a very nervous disposition. It is not a tram, but a cable car, and was built by a Swiss company in 1888, when it had a steam engine. It winds up from Central at a neck-twisting angle, among the skyscrapers, with astonishing panoramic views of the harbor and Kowloon.

Trams, real trams, run along the flat, northern shore of Hong Kong Island, and are probably the cheapest way of seeing the amazing city. They stop very frequently, and are the favorite method of short-distance city travel. There was a move to get rid of them in the 1970s as they were not modern enough, but fortunately they were saved and carry a lot of people who would otherwise crowd into the buses and MTR. The fare is shown inside the tram, and you put money into a box as you leave.

Road

There is a dense network of bus routes all over the territory, and if you have plenty of time, this is an excellent way to view street life. The fares are usually displayed both at the bus stops and inside the buses. Put the correct change in the box when you board.

For a more comfortable and faster ride, there are minibuses, which stop when flagged down although they keep to fixed routes if they are green and more-or-less fixed routes if they are red. Like the big buses, they require exact change, and charge higher prices. The terminals of each line and the boxes inside the buses have the prices displayed; they change somewhat through the journey as the distance you can go gets shorter, so if you are in doubt, look questioningly at the driver. To stop a minibus in the place you want, shout "*Yau lok!*" In the amazingly condensed Chinese language it means "There is someone wanting to get off!"

Taxis are quite good value. They are red in the urban area, a bit cheaper and green in the New Territories, and blue on Lantau. Tipping is not compulsory but it is appreciated. Some taxi drivers talk, but many do not expect to. Their familiarity with English is not great, and it may be difficult to make yourself understood, so it's a good plan to have the written Chinese version of the address you are visiting to show. However, there are usually helpful people around who will interpret for you if you're stuck.

It is not advisable to rent a car unless you have to travel extensively in the New Territories. Public transportation, including taxis, is so plentiful and cheap, the roads so congested, and one-way systems so complicated, that for most short-term visitors it would be a nightmare.

SHOPPING

It is something of a cliché that Hong Kong is a shoppers' paradise, but like all clichés, it is true! It used to be a place for the cheap and cheerful, but now every kind of product is available from dirt cheap to seriously expensive. Whether you like browsing in the street markets or sauntering through the marble malls, your taste can be indulged. Winter sales (late December to February) and summer sales (July to September) are good times to shop for expensive items, as major discounts are available for the avid shopper. The Hong Kong Tourism Board is concerned that there should be good service throughout the spectrum of shopping experiences, and they reward local enterprises that provide it, with Hong Kong Awards for Services.

The main shopping areas in Hong Kong are Central, Causeway Bay, and Stanley on Hong Kong Island, and the length of Nathan Road and neighboring streets in Kowloon. There are some other areas worth exploring. Near the airport on Tsing Yi Island, there is Maritime Square, which combines old and new in two hundred shops and restaurants. Ap Lei Chau is an island just off Aberdeen, where discount furniture and clothing are available. All the towns have their own mini-malls, stores, and markets.

It's important to compare prices, as there is a lot of competition between stores, and you will kick yourself if you find the same item at a lower price just next door to the store you have patronized! Check also that electrical goods have international guarantees. Many stores offer packing and postal service, with insurance, which is undoubtedly the safest and most convenient way of getting your treasures home.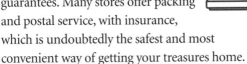

Prices are often not fixed, but prolonged haggling isn't Hong Kong style. In the cheaper markets, you may get a slight discount if you buy two items, but generally they are cheap enough not to bother. In more high-class stores, it's worth looking dubious when you are quoted a price, and asking if they can't give you a discount, or make a better price. In the electronics or jewelry shops this usually works quite well. You can also use your knowledge of other shops' prices to beat them down.

Most shops are open daily, 10:00 a.m. to 7:00 p.m. Supermarkets open 9:00 a.m. to 8:00 p.m. Shops in the busy retail areas of Causeway Bay and Tsimshatsui (or Tsim Sha Tsui) tend to open and close later (11:00 a.m. to as late as 9:30 p.m.). Banks are open Monday to Friday 9:00 a.m. to 4:30 p.m., Saturday 9:00 a.m. to 12:30 p.m.

The Malls

Hong Kong has several beautifully designed multistory malls, which have all you need under one roof. Pacific Place, the International Finance Centre Mall, The Landmark in Central, and Festival Walk in Kowloon are just some of these. In them you will find the famous names, with international designers, all popular with visitors and locals alike. If you start to flag, there are stylish coffee bars and fine restaurants to restore your energy. The biggest and brightest malls often host fashion shows, showcasing the very latest trends from around the world.

Department Stores

World-class department stores from many countries can be found all over the territory. In Central, Lane Crawford, Wing On, and Sincere are three locally owned stores. Among top foreign firms are Sogo, Seibu, and Mitsukoshi from Japan and Marks & Spencer from Britain. These have mouthwatering food halls as well as floors of fashions and housewares. Particularly good value are the China Products and Yue Hwa stores, where you can find a huge range of Chinese goods.

Factory Outlets

Many of Hong Kong's expatriates have discovered the joys of factory outlets. They sell overruns and stock surplus to requirements, which are all good quality, as well as samples and quality-control rejects that are less than perfect. It's important to examine the goods carefully for obvious defects.

Most of the outlets specialize in women's clothes, and you can find silk, cashmere, cotton, linen, and knitwear. Apart from the very good bargains to be had, the principal reason for their popularity is that the sizes are Western and therefore more generous than the average Oriental sizes. Some factories produce clothing for famous designer labels, and you usually find the labels cut out. There are a few outlets with men's and children's clothes too. Some specialize in porcelain, furniture, or candles, and it's a good plan to get the Hong Kong Tourist Board's leaflet on factory shopping. There are numerous clothing outlets in Pedder Building, Pedder Street, Central, and in Granville Road, Tsimshatsui, Kowloon. Most of the best ones are concentrated on the Kaiser Estate, a large warehouse area in Hung Hom, near Kowloon Railway Station. Bus 5C from the Star Ferry will take you there—alight at Ma Tau Wai Road.

Markets

There are market halls in every urban center in Hong Kong, with a variety of fresh foods, cheap clothing, and housewares. There are also several areas of street stalls, notably "The Lanes" in Central, and Jardine's Bazaar in Causeway Bay. The open-air Night Market in Yau Ma Tei and Stanley Market cater mostly to foreigners and tourists. Ladies' Market on Tung Choi Street in Mong Kok is a popular street market with cheap clothing, accessories, and housewares. There is a specialist Flower Market near Prince Edward Station in Kowloon, and the Jade Market (see below).

Art and Handicrafts

China Products, Yue Hwa, and CAC (Chinese Arts and Crafts) have a good range of Chinese art and handicrafts. Shanghai Tang is a chain store specializing in high-quality and unusual products. Hollywood Road in Central is the hub of the antiques trade, and you can find silk and embroidery, porcelain, and metalwork.

Jade

The Chinese character for jade touches upon the three adjectives it represents—pure, noble, and beautiful. The Chinese have always prized jade, and the four hundred stalls in the Jade Market in Yau Ma Tei have every type and style of jade ornament, from rings to elaborately carved Buddhas. Colors range from white to green so dark it is almost black. Top-quality jade is pure, translucent green, cold to the touch, and very expensive. Most pieces have a yellow tinge but any cloudy, gray, or brown tints are less valued. It is regarded as a protective stone, and babies are often given a jade ornament.

Tailoring
Hong Kong is famous for the speed, good value, and craftsmanship of its tailoring. There are numerous tailors, both Chinese and Indian, in the streets off Nathan Road in Tsimshatsui, Kowloon. They can make anything from silk Chinese dresses (*cheung sam*) to business suits, or a copy of one of your favorite garments.

Jewelry and Watches
High-quality jewelry and watch shops abound in Hong Kong. The prices aren't rock-bottom, but the quality and variety are astounding.

Electrical and Electronic Goods
Hong Kong is gadget-crazy, and you can find many good bargains in this sector. Hundreds of stores sell cameras, household gadgets, audiovisual equipment, and computers. The Golden Computer

Arcade and the Golden Computer Centre near Sham Shuit Po Station are crammed with hardware and software stores, though the incredible bargains of yesteryear are no longer available since police crackdowns on piracy.

Optical Goods

Glasses and contact lenses are reasonably priced and can be made astonishingly quickly in Hong Kong. The optical shops stock a huge range of frames. Many of them have a resident optician who can see you right away, is very professional, and can provide you with a prescription within minutes.

INTERNATIONAL ENTERTAINMENT

You name it, you've got it. Hong Kong has always had more than its fair share of shows and concerts as Western players passed through it on their way to China, so top orchestras, theater and dance groups, and solo artistes are no strangers to its shores. There are fifteen attractive cultural venues of varying size and capacity.

Every year there is an International Film Festival, with entries from over forty countries, and the Hong Kong Arts Festival, one of the most exciting events of its type in the Asia–Pacific region. Pan-Asian cultural events like Legends of China and the New Vision Arts Festival are held in alternate years. Hong Kong has its own ballet and other dance companies, as well as a Philharmonic Orchestra, a Chinese Orchestra, and a Sinfonietta.

If you are more interested in places to relax, there are bars featuring live music in all the top hotels, the Fringe Club has comedy and jazz, and there are plenty of clubs with dancing and music.

International movies are popular. There are some smart modern multiplex cinemas, and new movies reach Hong Kong very quickly.

There are numerous arts and antique galleries, centered on Hollywood Road in Central, as well as special exhibitions.

Details of special events can be found at the Hong Kong Tourist Association's Web site, www.hkta.org.

CHINESE-STYLE ENTERTAINMENT
Apart from the Hong Kong Chinese Orchestra, there are several small musical groups that play Chinese music.

Cantonese opera is the best-known homegrown entertainment, and it is worthwhile sampling it, because there is nothing like it in Western culture. The Hong Kong Tourist Association has a two-hour introduction to this sort of opera for foreigners as well as a fascinating four-hour introduction to the make-up and performance.

For foreign visitors eager to get a taste of Hong Kong culture, the Tourist Association also provides many tours and introductions to diverse cultural aspects of the place.

DAYS OUT AND EXCURSIONS

The city area is endlessly interesting to explore, as there is still a fascinating juxtaposition of the ultramodern and the traditional. The Tourist Association publishes leaflets of walks in and around the city. But if you are yearning for some peace, there are several ways of escaping from the buzz. An incredible 40 percent of Hong Kong's territory is Country Park, and you can find yourself with a large view of greenery and woodland and not a single building. There are some stunningly beautiful beaches in Hong Kong, with golden sands and craggy cliffs. The waters are, alas, polluted by factory and rural effluent coming down the Pearl River, which debouches to the west, but the government has put a lot of effort and money into cleaning the beaches and keeping a close eye on the pollution count, which is published for every beach. The cleanest beaches tend to be on the south and east sides of the territory, away from the main course of the water from the Pearl River.

Hong Kong Island

If the weather is clear, the best place to start is the Peak. This is the tallest mountain on Hong Kong Island, and is best approached by the Peak Tram (see Getting Around, above). From the top of the tram there is a level walk around the mountain, which offers wide views over the busy city on one side and over green slopes and the South China Sea on the other. It takes nearly two hours if you go at the leisurely pace it deserves. Part of it is a fitness trail, if you feel in need of more exercise. Tougher types can climb up from the tram to the top of the Peak, where there is an observation table and the gardens of an old governor's residence, long since burned down.

Hong Kong Park is an oasis of green in the heart of the urban landscape of Central. It includes an aviary, a greenhouse, the Hong Kong Visual Arts Centre, and the Flagstaff House Museum of Tea Ware. On a near-vertical site, it is a great example

of modern garden design and facilities blending with the natural landscape. Just above the park are the zoo and botanical gardens, also pleasantly green in the middle of the city. There are some interesting animals and colorful birds, and several places to sit and enjoy nature.

Ocean Park is a lively theme park with pandas, dolphin shows, and a striking aquarium. It has huge views over the South China Sea and a spectacular

cable car ride across the cliffs. Included in your ticket is a visit to the Middle Kingdom, which is a re-creation of an old Chinese village, with acrobatic, juggling, and magic shows as well as traditional snacks and drinks. This makes a rather expensive but very enjoyable day out for the whole family.

Aberdeen is the oldest habitation on Hong Kong Island, and is the center of a large fishing industry. Previously most of the inhabitants lived in boats in the harbor but most of these have been rehoused in the usual high-rise blocks and a smart marina has taken their place. The famous "floating restaurants" serve seafood and other Chinese dishes in Aberdeen harbor.

Repulse Bay and Stanley are two settlements on the south of the island. The ride along the road to

Stanley via Repulse Bay has wonderful views. Repulse Bay has a large beach, which is kept very clean, a replica of a 1920s hotel, and a Buddhist temple next to the beach.

Stanley has one of the most popular market areas, for foreigners in particular. Clothing and handicrafts are available at very competitive prices. Threatened with closure a few years back, the market traders and outraged shoppers mounted so strong a protest that they won the day.

Shek O and Big Wave Bay are two seaside villages, on the west side of Hong Kong Island, that have good beaches.

Elsewhere, in Kowloon and the New Territories, in many of the outlying islands and in Macao, you will find an enormous variety of attractive scenery, and things to do and see. All details are available from the Hong Kong tourist office.

NIGHTLIFE

When asked about nightlife, a local Chinese shook his head. "We go to bed around 10:30 because we have to be up early and go to work." Be that as it may, the visitor will find plenty of places to go in the evening. After a happy hour drink (typically available from 5:00 p.m. to 8:00 p.m.) and a good dinner, take a stroll around the Temple Street night market to check out the fake watches and Westernsized clothing. Extra Extra Large in Hong Kong seems to be about Medium in the West! You can even get your fortune told here. Then, for more refreshment and entertainment, there are several good bars—including many karaoke bars—on the island in the Lan Kwai Fong (LKF) and SoHo areas. LKF has such an astonishing variety of bars and discos that you can stagger from one to the next all night and never go to the same one twice. You may find girls wanting you to buy drinks for them in discos—but beware, they are mostly not casual pickups but professional hostesses.

If you are looking for company but don't dance, the many girlie bars of Tsimshatsui and Wanchai can provide you with an escort. Some of these bars are topless, and at all of them a hostess will join you for a pretty expensive drink—and ask for another every ten or fifteen minutes. Snacks are not free, and even if you don't eat them, you'll probably be charged. The drink prices, although posted somewhere in the bar by law, tend to escalate as the evening progresses.

Hotel coffee shops are open twenty-four hours, and there are night buses, so if you want to be out until the early hours, food and transportation should be no problem. Taxis charge a post-midnight supplement.

SPORTS AND EXERCISE

Hong Kong people are not, on the whole, very interested in sports. The lack of space for fields and pitches means that few children have the chance to play the sports, such as football of all kinds, baseball, and cricket, that Western children are used to playing. Most children will be taught how to swim, and may play basketball, volleyball, or table tennis. Golf is popular, but the public courses are usually jam-packed, and the private ones are extremely expensive.

Adults take exercise either by going to a gym or by walking, including hiking in the country parks, where there are often fitness trails. Traditionally, the Chinese get up early and go to an open area, if possible up a hill, to do *tai chi*. You may join these groups in their hypnotic exercises. They tend to attract older members of the community who, according to statistics, remain flexible and fit and have a good life expectancy. Expatriates tend to join recreation clubs, which have swimming pools, tennis courts, and other leisure pursuits.

FOOD
& DRINK

Hong Kong prides itself on the huge range of cuisines available in its four thousand restaurants catering to all budgets and tastes. Until twenty years ago, most locals would eat Cantonese food at home or when out, but the internationalization of the city has caused an upsurge in the popularity of other styles of cooking and eating.

CHINESE FOOD

Cantonese

The Cantonese regard their food as the best in the world, and even other Chinese acknowledge its flavor and variety. Some say Cantonese cooking is to China what French cooking is to Europe.

Easy emigration from the New Territories in the 1960s and '70s has led to the proliferation of so-called Chinese restaurants in many parts of the world, which produce a travesty of traditional dishes in order to please the local palates. True Cantonese cooking is as far from the *chopsuey* (which means "miscellaneous bits") and *chowmein* of Britain or

Canada as French cooking is from bottled sauces with French names. A very un-Chinese meal appears in Canada as "Chinese smorgasbord," and tends to consist of a buffet of dank metal tubs containing meat and vegetables cooked hours earlier.

The good Chinese cook shops twice a day to ensure the freshness of the ingredients, though frozen and convenience foods are catching on in Hong Kong as everywhere. Fresh produce markets abound, and are a vital part of any area.

The Cantonese say that they eat "everything with four legs except tables and chairs, and everything in the sky except planes," or "anything that walks, swims, crawls, or flies with its back to heaven." This all-inclusive attitude leads to some bizarre and, to Westerners, repugnant recipes, including rice worms, civet cat's paws, snails, and snakes. At home,  however, the usual food is not so eccentric. A meal for a family of four might consist of three courses with rice. The courses do not succeed each other as in a Western meal, but are put on the table as soon as they are cooked. Food is for the most part cooked by stir- or deep-frying, which means that it is done quickly and should be eaten immediately, while crisp and fresh. Raw food, except for fruit, is viewed with suspicion, and salad is not on the Cantonese menu. Even lettuce and watercress are lightly fried. This is a prudent health measure, as animal (and until recently human) waste is used on vegetable gardens. Most of the fresh produce comes from the mainland, where this tradition still tends to apply.

A typical meal will have at least two kinds of protein, served at more or less the same time. Fish and seafood are very popular with Hongkongers, and were the staple protein of the original fishing communities, but they are more expensive today. Pork is the meat of choice—in fact the word for "meat" in Cantonese means pork—with beef coming second. Lamb is not used in Cantonese cuisine, as sheep do not thrive in the subtropical south of China, and the flavor is regarded as "too strong" and unpleasant. Poultry is well liked, with chicken being common everywhere, and duck or goose used for many popular dishes. Bean curd is another important source of protein, and strict Buddhist vegetarians make many dishes with it.

The Chinese traditionally believed that it was unseemly (and possibly dangerous) to have knives at the table, which is why everything is cut to bite size. Chopsticks are of ancient origin, long antedating the forks of Western cuisine. Once you have witnessed their expert use they will never seem awkward and limited again, but it does take time and practice to become adept. Chinese cooking therefore starts from the premise of small pieces, which makes stir-frying such an ideal method. It combines keeping as much as possible of the food's freshness and flavor with speed of preparation. For extra flavor, very strong sauces are used in sparing quantities.

The Cantonese staple is rice. So central is it to the diet that, instead of "How are you?" as a greeting from someone you know, they will ask "Have you eaten rice yet?" Every home will have a rice cooker, a slow electric cooker where a certain amount of water is put with the rice. Once cooked, it keeps hot with a thermostatic control. Steamed or boiled rice is served with all meals. At breakfast, congee, or *juk*, may be eaten; this is watery rice gruel, spiced up with sauce and served with small pieces of chicken, peanuts, and preserved eggs (see below). Modern, busy Cantonese tend either to go out for breakfast or to grab a bowl of cereal or slice of toast like their Western counterparts.

Hundred-Year-Old Eggs

These eggs, which you will see for sale in the market or quartered on a plate in a hotel breakfast buffet, do have an ancient look to them. They are in fact only about a hundred days old. They should be duck eggs, and they are preserved in potash and salt. The white turns dark gray, and the yolk blackish. They taste salty, but not old!

Typical dishes on the Cantonese menu would include chicken and cashew nuts, sliced beef in black bean sauce, pork with mushrooms, and fried bean curd and vegetables. A green vegetable would usually be served as well, either steamed with garlic and ginger or served in oyster sauce.

Choi sum is the most typical Hong Kong vegetable, also known as mustard greens. *Pak choi* (or *bok choi*) and Tientsin cabbage are also popular. One of the most delicious vegetables is *dao foo*, or pea leaves, which come into season in November. Cooked vegetables often come in longer pieces, which are held in the chopsticks and nibbled.

Bird's Nest Soup

Most people think "bird's nest soup" is a fanciful name, and are incredulous when they hear that this soup is actually made from bird's nests. Only one type of bird, the swiftlet of Southeast Asia, makes nests suitable for this soup. The nests are made of the bird's saliva. Luckily for the swiftlets, the nests are hard to reach. Gatherers have to climb up inside dangerous caves, balancing on bamboo poles. The flavor of the soup is subtle, and it is usually accompanied by a sweet vinegar to spice it up. It is the soup's reputation as an aphrodisiac that makes it so popular, as with many rare and unusual foods in China.

Soup is sometimes served, especially in winter, but it does not come at the beginning of the meal. Snake soup is a specialty of winter cooking, meant to help build up resistance to the cold.

Desserts were not part of ordinary Cantonese culture, but the meal will often end with fruit, most probably an orange. The Cantonese eat more oranges and drink more orange juice than any other ethnic group.

Dim Sum

Dim sum is literally translated as "touching the heart," which implies that you can eat "to your heart's content." It refers to a meal taken any time between mid-morning and early afternoon. The dishes are piled in bamboo steamers and brought around on trolleys from table to table, usually by stern, middle-aged women, who shout their particular specialty's name as they pass around the room. The dishes consist mainly of two or three steamed or fried buns, dumplings, or spring rolls with a variety of fillings—meat and prawns as well as vegetables.

You can usually order green vegetables and rice dishes as well, but you do not need these to make a satisfying brunch. Tea is the standard drink, and the morning *dim sum* outing is often referred to as *yum cha*—drinking tea.

The price of the meal is traditionally calculated by counting the dishes left on the customer's table. However, nowadays many *dim sum* restaurants record the dishes on a card at the table.

Hakka

The Hakkas were latecomers to southern China, and settled in the most steep and arid areas of Guangdong and Hong Kong, a long way from the growing areas. As food could not be procured fresh twice a day, it had to be preserved, so the cuisine is not in the "just-picked" style of the Cantonese.

Two traditional Hakka recipes are salt-baked chicken, supposed to be baked inside a heap of hot salt, but often just cooked in salty water, and beef-ball soup, a clear broth with lettuce and beef balls.

Beijing

Probably the best-known Beijing dish is Beijing or Peking Duck, which consists of thin slices of roast duck wrapped with plum sauce and spring onion in a thin pancake, eaten with the fingers. Beijing cuisine contains largely wheat-based food, such as noodles and buns, which makes the northerners taller and larger than the Cantonese.

Szechuan

Western Chinese food is hot and spicy, and the Cantonese have learned to enjoy it. *Ma poh dao foo,* or "old lady's bean curd"—minced pork and bean curd in a hot and tasty sauce—is a particularly popular dish.

Formal Meals and Festivals

For formal dining (see Entertaining, in Chapter 5), certain dishes have ritual significance because of their names, which sound like lucky phrases. Spring dinners are often held at and around Lunar New Year, and one dish you will always find at these is moss and dried oysters. Its Cantonese name is *Fat choi ho si*, which translates as "Good business in the New Year." Steamed fish, which is nearly always on the menu of a banquet, has no special name, but the word for "fish" and the word for "surplus" sound the same. Mushrooms, pork leg, and duck's feet mean "To be successful everywhere."

Special food and drink for festivals also sometimes have verbal or visual references to other things. The moon cakes cooked for the Mid-Autumn or Lantern Festival, for example, contain a whole hard-boiled egg, which looks like the full moon. They are also stamped with a lucky written character.

DRINKS

With Chinese food, the universal drink is Chinese tea. This usually comes free with the meal, and in most restaurants is not jasmine-flavored, but is *ching cha*—ordinary tea. When your teapot is empty, it is customary to leave the lid half open so the waiter will fill it up with hot water again. It is traditionally thought bad for the health to drink ice-cold drinks; if plain water is ordered, it will often be brought hot.

There are of course many different types of tea, and there are fascinating specialist shops with all the varieties on display. One that the visitor might come across is oolong tea, served very strong in tiny cups, after a meal. It has the same style and kick as an espresso coffee. Jasmine tea, or *heung pin*, can also be ordered in most restaurants.

It is customary for waiters or for your Chinese hosts to replenish glasses or teacups from time to time, and they are traditionally thanked by tapping with the fingertips on the tabletop, so that the flow of conversation is not interrupted.

Most of the population worldwide has been thoroughly saturated with Coke, Sprite, and other soft fizzy drinks, and Hong Kong is no exception. But there is also a taste for orange juice, the fresher the better, and you can buy small cartons of different fruit juices everywhere.

Light beer is a cheap, pleasant, refreshing drink with or without food. The locally made San Miguel, and Tsingtao, from a northern Chinese factory started by Germans, are as popular as Heineken and Carlsberg.

At a banquet, brandy is often the drink of choice. Those who do not wish to quaff glassfuls of it are offered Sprite to dilute it with—not the most respectful way of treating a four-star drink, but acceptable to Eastern palates. At a traditional banquet so-called "Chinese wine" would be served as a digestive after the meal. This is a distillation from rice, millet, or other grains, often flavored with herbs and flowers. *Mao tai* is probably the best-known, based on millet. It's fiery, with a strong flavor and a 70 percent alcohol content. *Siu ching* wine is yellow, with a flavor rather like dry sherry, and is often used in Cantonese cooking.

Grape-based wine and other imported drinks are freely available in Hong Kong, and can be found in supermarkets and specialist shops as well as most restaurants. Similarly, Western-style tea and coffee are found in the many coffee shops around town.

chapter eight

BUSINESS BRIEFING

WHY DO BUSINESS IN HONG KONG?

The head of the Hong Kong Economic and Trade Office in Europe said in 2003 that Hong Kong people expected to have the world's freest economy, the lowest crime and corruption rates in the region, busiest container port, most popular international airport, busiest air-cargo hub, most independent judiciary, strongest legal system, and widest guaranteed freedoms.

Hong Kong's geographical position means that it is daytime there when it is night in North America and early morning in Europe. This means that firms with offices in all three places can actually work twenty-four hours on certain types of projects. This can be especially useful in the areas of financial services and communications.

HONG KONG'S ECONOMY

Hong Kong has long had a thriving free-market economy. It is a region with few natural resources, and trade—originally with Britain and China—has been its lifeblood. Food and raw materials are imported. Imports and exports, including re-exports, exceed GDP in dollar value. In 2004 Hong Kong was named the world's freest economy for the tenth consecutive year by the Heritage Foundation/*Wall Street Journal*'s "Index of Economic Freedom." Even though the rest of the region's economics has been tightly controlled during the last year, Hong Kong has managed to remain free, and to maintain its minimal regulations and low taxes.

Hong Kong has always had extensive trade and investment ties with the mainland, serving as the world's window on the China trade. But since the return to Chinese rule, economic ties have become even stronger. There was fear that Hong Kong would lose out when China became a member of the World Trade Organization in 2001, but this does not appear to have been the case. Hong Kong is still seen as the gateway to China. Many manufacturing centers have moved to the mainland, where labor and production costs are low, but typically the head offices remain in Hong Kong, mainly because of the rule of law. However, manufacturing has given way over the past fifteen years to services, with financial services being a particularly strong sector.

In 2003, the economy was adversely affected by SARS, a virus that killed three hundred people in Hong Kong and several thousand more worldwide. Warnings about SARS brought Hong Kong's tourism and aviation industries to a standstill. Unemployment suddenly rocketed, reaching a record high of 8.7 percent. The real estate market, which had already plummeted after 1997, crashed further. However, the economy has made a strong recovery since then. Consumer confidence and an upbeat stock market have both helped. The most significant areas of growth will continue to be foreign trade and tourism.

The Closer Economic Partnership Arrangement (CEPA) with the mainland government, signed in June 2003, gives Hong Kong distinct advantages over foreign rivals. As China relaxes travel restrictions between the mainland and Hong Kong, tourists from the mainland are becoming the economy's single largest source of growth.

BEFORE YOU START
Hong Kong is all about business, and business is the language most of Hong Kong speaks. Because of this, life is made easy for businesspeople, from the hotels with great business facilities, to cheap and effective communications technology, to restaurants close to or in office blocks specializing

in catering to the hungry negotiator. However, there are a number of pitfalls in negotiating with Hong Kong Chinese businesspeople that you should be aware of. Don't let the superficially Western style fool you into believing that Hongkongers will act and react as Westerners do.

Do remember that, although Chinese business-people are eager to acquire Western technology and products, they are inherently biased against foreigners. If they can do business with a Chinese, they will. The next best thing to being Chinese is, however, to behave as much like them as you can.

Business Hours

Hong Kong businesses work Monday through Friday, and often on Saturday mornings as well. Generally, the business day starts at 9:00 a.m., but breakfast meetings are not uncommon. Lunches are sometimes long, and may start at 12 noon. Most businesses close officially at 5:00 p.m., although staff may often stay later. Bear in mind that Chinese New Year and many other holidays are bad times to try and see people in Hong Kong, as many of them will be taking time off.

Appointments

Appointments should be made as far in advance as possible, and should be attended scrupulously on time. It is better to be early for an appointment than late, so leave plenty of time and allow for traffic congestion on the roads and even on the sidewalks. If you are late, you should apologize profusely, even if it was unavoidable, as it is regarded as very disrespectful. Be generous and gracious to anyone else who is late.

Who's Who?

Endeavor to become aware of the positions, status, and family relationship of each member of the Hong Kong negotiating team. Most businesses are small and family-owned. Even larger businesses will employ members of the same family. Age is still respected, so an older family member may well be present as a figurehead at the meeting. So it's often not appropriate to address all conversation and presentations to the senior negotiator. He or she may be a ceremonial figure, and the more junior staff will be expected to filter the relevant information to him or her.

However democratic you wish to be, paying close attention to the hierarchy is essential. It would not be appropriate to listen attentively to a secretary or to interrupt an older person. Greeting junior staff, and courtesies such as "please" and "thank you" are always welcome, but overfamiliarity will make it difficult to maintain your authority. Beware of delegating tasks of any kind, since asking employees to do something that they regard as beneath them, or outside their domain, is a breach of protocol. An inappropriate request will be quietly ignored, since it would not be right for an employee to react with indignation.

Names

Again, formality is the keynote in addressing business counterparts. In Chinese names, the surname comes first, so it would be appropriate to call Liu Kam-fai "Mr. Liu." Often a Chinese will take a Western name as well. You may see a name written thus: "Stephen LIU Kam-fai." Most married women keep their maiden names, but sometimes will write both maiden and married names: "Grace MA CHAK Ka-lei." This can be puzzling to foreigners, but in this case it would be fine to call her Ms. or Miss Ma. It is not wrong to address a married woman as Miss, since she keeps her maiden name. In China it was customary to use Madam before a woman's surname, but this is a little old-fashioned now. Titles, like Professor and Doctor, are important to their holders, so make a point of using them.

When you know someone well, they may ask you to call them by their surname only, or by a Western name like Stephen. They may refer to their colleagues by their surnames only. Chinese given names are not commonly used, even within the family.

Business Cards

Business cards are an essential part of Hong Kong life, so make sure you have some printed when you are there and before you make contact. It is best to have English on one side and Chinese on the other. Your card should include your title and name, the name and address of your company, and your contact telephone numbers. Most cards feature the logo of the company as well. Because the "chop," or seal, of a person or a business has always had prominence in Chinese culture, the logo has now replaced it as a symbol of the firm and it may be more memorable than a name. It is an intrinsic part of the company's identity.

You will need to have your surname (at least) transliterated into Chinese characters. This is a guide to pronunciation, although it may sound very different from your idea of your surname. Because Chinese surnames are one syllable, the first syllable of your name will be what you are addressed as. For example, Mrs. McFarlane would be "Mrs. Mak," Mr. Williamson would be "Mr. Wai," Dr. Yudkin, "Dr. Yau," and so on.

Getting It Right

It is important that the person who chooses your transliteration is scholarly enough to do it well. A slip-up in a character can result in something ridiculous, unlucky, or rude. Someone whose name was transliterated to (Wai) Ka-si found to his consternation that the characters printed meant "furniture" instead of the lofty intended meaning, "encourager of thought."

The exchange of business cards is an important preliminary ritual in Hong Kong. If someone presents you with theirs, and you do not offer one in return, they will feel that you are not interested in the acquaintance, or that you are not important enough for them to deal with. Business cards are presented and received with two hands. This gives face to both parties. It would be very disrespectful to take a card with just one hand, and if you offer one in this way, you are thought to be dismissive of your own company. When receiving someone's card, make a show of examining it for a few moments; then carefully place it into your card case or on the table in front of you.

What to Wear

Hong Kong is still conservative in dress. Men wear dark suits with shirts and ties in relatively sober shades, and women in senior positions tend to wear dark or subdued colors, conservative necklines, and long sleeves. Skirts of a decorous length and trousers are equally acceptable. You cannot go wrong if you imitate this style.

Gift Giving

It is customary to bring a gift to your Hong Kong counterparts. The type and style of the gift should be considered carefully, and it should be attractively wrapped. It is considered rude not to wrap a gift. Acceptable gifts include specialties from your home country, handicrafts, and coffee-table books. You can expect to receive a gift in return. Hosting a banquet (see Chapter 5) counts as a gift, and if your Hong Kong hosts do this for you, it is appropriate to host one for them. In the fairly unlikely event of being invited to a Hongkonger's home, you should take a wrapped bottle of Scotch or brandy, and some nicely presented fruit, cookies, or candy.

More important are the no-nos: clocks are an intimation of mortality; green hats are marks of a cuckold; blue wrapping paper is not favored because blue is associated with death.

As with business cards, gifts should be given and received with two hands. It is not considered polite to unwrap a gift in front of the giver, as it would mark you as impatient and greedy. Thank the giver, and put it to one side to be opened later.

At Chinese New Year (see Festivals and Holidays, in Chapter 3), if you happen to be in Hong Kong, it would be fitting to distribute *laisee* to unmarried junior staff who know you and have helped you. Chinese New Year cards and sometimes Christmas cards too will be sent to all contacts, and will be expected in return.

DIPLOMACY

Don't go straight into business talk when you first meet your contacts. It is best to get to know your counterparts first and create a calm, relaxed mood. A little polite conversation on a neutral topic is always a good bet. Keeping off politics, Chinese politics in particular, is certainly recommended. Food is to the Chinese what the weather is to the English. Praise for local cuisine will be appreciated (but it may be a good idea to find out if your contact is Cantonese first) and some interested questions about health, festivals, or the races, but personal lives and plans are off-limits until you know someone pretty well.

Although accustomed to Western openness and frankness, many Chinese prefer to be circumspect, and will probably appreciate it if you are too.

It doesn't pay to try the hard sell or other aggressive business moves. Direct questions may elicit less information than hints or indirect approaches. In particular, do not come out with any awkward or unpleasant facts in public, and reserve this sort of frankness for private conversation. This relates to the significance of preserving someone's status in front of their staff. Showing anger and annoyance is not productive in business or social meetings with Chinese. It actually puts you somewhat at a disadvantage, because it shows a lack of control. You will lose a lot of points if you lose your temper.

Face

Understanding the concept of "face" is essential to succeeding in Hong Kong's business culture. A person's reputation and standing rest on the concept of their "saving face," and causing them embarrassment or loss of self-possession, even unintentionally, can be disastrous for business negotiations. A person's actions reflect not only on his or her company, but also on the family, and any other groups of which he is a member.

Remember that you will lose face if you become angry, irritable, or upset. And, since your counterpart wishes to save face, he will not want to be associated with your lack of it. Speak calmly and present your arguments and materials in a positive and modest way. Conflict should never be apparent. Modesty is greatly prized, and conflicts with the Western idea of selling yourself.

Ways of Thinking

Western-trained businesspeople may well be logical thinkers, guided by objective and even abstract factors. This will be true of Hongkongers with further education and more experience abroad. But the majority of Chinese in business are associative thinkers. They tend to go on "feel" and "hunch" rather than facts and figures. Their faith in the philosophy of a particular company or group will probably be a central factor in their thinking. There is emphasis on the whole rather than the individual, harmony rather than fragmentation.

NEGOTIATION

It is advantageous to keep the same team throughout the negotiations. That way, a feeling of trust and respect can be fostered. And since  age is revered, it helps a lot if your chief negotiator is in his or her fifties.

It is a good plan to have several alternative options, in order to give your Chinese counterparts room to maneuver. They can then retain face while rejecting or altering some of your suggestions.

Don't assume that the word "yes" means agreement. It is used as a marker to show that the listener has understood what you are saying. Likewise, if you don't hear the word "no," it doesn't mean that there has been agreement. The Chinese will not use "no" directly, but will use some phrase such as "I'll think about it," or "Perhaps."

Negotiations can be very slow and protracted, with extensive attention to detail. Another point to note is that the Chinese negotiating team may request a large discount toward the end of the negotiations, which may be referred to as a "compromise," so factor this in before you start.

There are also many issues that can be resolved by respecting your Chinese counterparts' belief in *feng shui* (see Chapter 3).

TEA

Don't underestimate its importance! You should always accept an offer of a cup of tea, as it shows a willingness to participate in the negotiations. When you are served, wait for the host to drink first. Teacups are useful visual aids; your cup may represent your company, for example, and the position of the cups may indicate the closeness of the two companies to an agreement.

THE RULE OF LAW

The rule of law is extremely important. It provides clarity and certainty so that people can plan their lives—you know what the law is and know that any changes to it will be made in accordance with the rule of law. All government decisions will be made in accordance with checks and balances, so executives cannot abuse their power, and government and its decision-making process will be transparent. The police will also be subject to law, and therefore should not abuse their powers. Individuals are guaranteed a fair, unbiased hearing and trial.

The rule of law is the best alternative to the rule of the whim of whomever is in power, whether it be a dictator or the tyranny of the majority. The outcome in modern liberal democracies is that basic human rights are respected.

Since the handover to China, Hong Kong's freedoms have been guaranteed by the Basic Law, which promises "one country, two systems," so the previous capitalist system and way of life should remain unchanged for fifty years. One of the main reasons for business staying in Hong Kong instead of moving into the mainland is the rule of law, which has always played a vital role in Hong Kong's success, and will continue to be essential for its future. Any tampering with or "reinterpretation" of the Basic Law might jeopardize this, which is why the Hong Kong lawmakers are so vigilant.

To quote Ms. Elsie Leung, Hong Kong's Secretary for Justice, 'The rule of law begins with individuals and their right to seek the protection of the courts, in which justice is administered by impartial judges. It protects the freedom of individuals to manage their affairs without fear of arbitrary interference by the Government or the improper influence of the rich and powerful. Its starting point is the individual but it encompasses the whole of society."

Hong Kong has had the British common law system since the beginning, although certain ordinances make provision for traditional Chinese law as well. Particularly valued are the law of contract and intellectual property law, so important in the world of business. There are numerous large international and local law firms in Hong Kong, with long experience in dealing with other Asian countries. The legal system has a Court of Final Appeal (CFA), established at the handover, which is the ultimate arbiter of the exercise of common law in Hong Kong.

BUSINESS AND GOVERNMENT

The Hong Kong SAR Government actively supports business, and there are Economic and Trade Offices in eleven overseas locations that can provide a great deal of information before you arrive in the territory. The government is small and efficient, and is well known for its transparency and fairness. It rarely interferes in the business community, and both personal and corporate taxes are comparatively low and simple to calculate.

The Department of Trade and Industry offers a free service to people wishing to set up businesses, providing information on all government licenses, permits, certificates, and approvals relevant to business operation in Hong Kong. The Labour Department can give information on recruitment and human resource management, the Immigration Department on visas. Help with financing is available, and once your business is launched, you can get help with development and management.

TRADE FAIRS

Hong Kong's Trade Development Council organizes a great many trade fairs during the year. The venue, the Hong Kong Convention and Exhibition Centre, is beautifully located on the harborside, and is a large and well-appointed building.

The TDC also has a range of helpful links and a Web site to enable businessmen from abroad to make contact with Hong Kong companies. Over forty categories of goods and services are listed to help people find each other.

chapter nine

COMMUNICATING

GETTING BY IN ENGLISH

Visitors can usually get by with English in Hong Kong, although the education system emphasizes written English over spoken. It may be useful to write down names or questions if your speech is met with incomprehension. A few words of Cantonese will elicit gasps of surprise and lavish praise from the locals. With older speakers, if you can say more than a couple of phrases, the praise tends to die away. There is a slight suspicion of anyone who speaks the language too well—they might understand too much!

Even when English can be used there may be difficulties. There is a confusing grammatical tendency arising from the fact that in Chinese the answer to any statement is an affirmation or contradiction of the statement, for example, "You don't mean that, do you?"—the answer "Yes" would mean, for them, "Yes, you are right, I don't mean that" where English speakers would mean "Yes, I do mean that." So beware of yes and no!

Intonation is taught in English classes, but only

advanced speakers get it right. So be prepared to ask for several repetitions, and if necessary ask for something to be written down.

Hong Kong people like to talk, and even those with limited English will try their best to communicate. The accent tends to be strong, however, and it is sometimes very difficult for a foreigner with an untrained ear to distinguish what is being said. Bear in mind that Cantonese is a language of single syllables, most of which end in a vowel or a "stopped" vowel (like a glottal stop—imagine a London cockney saying "lot," "book," "rap," where the final consonant is not released). Hence English words ending with several consonants may well be rendered with only a passing nod to those required. Here are some common words that might fool a foreigner, where * stands for a glottal stop:

The word "Don't." *Do* shu* the door* sounds like "Do shut the door."

"How old are you?" said as "*How o* you?*" sounds like "How are you?"

The word "Help," said as *hel**, sounds like "Hell" (but receptionists seem to be taught to compensate by saying, *Can I help-t-you?*).

"Drink(s)" sounds like *dring* (*What dring you wan*?*)

In the local version of Cantonese, "n" and "l" are often confused, so you may be asked for a *pho lumber* (phone number). The final "s" or "sh" on a word may be pronounced with an *ee* sound afterward, which gave rise to the "joke Chinese" style of *washee clozee* for "wash clothes."

THE MEDIA

Hong Kong people are fond of their media. There is huge readership of the Chinese language press, although there may be a tendency for the racing pages to be of prime interest. There are two world-class English language newspapers, *The South China Morning Post* and *The Hong Kong Standard*, and a weekly magazine, *Spike* , which is popular with expatriates. The most influential Chinese language papers are *Ming Pao*, *The Apple Daily*, and *The Oriental Daily*. The stance of the first two is more understanding of than critical of Beijing, and *The Apple Daily*, originally forthright in its quest for truth in politics and exposure of scandal, has degenerated into a gossipy, semi-pornographic tabloid read more for sensationalism than truth.

RTHK is the government company that produces news and public information programs. There are four commercial television channels, "Pearl" (English) and "Jade" (Chinese) run by TVB, and "World" (English) and "Home" (Chinese) run by ATV. The English channels stick mainly to finance, lifestyle, and wildlife programs, with news in English and Mandarin. ATV is now controlled by a former senior propaganda official in China's People's Liberation Army and his Hong Kong associate. Additionally, Cable TV is available, carrying mainly movie, sports, and financial channels in both English and Chinese.

Hong Kong people have long recognized that the press is generally self-censoring. There is a tendency to look outside the territory for unbiased news stories, and CNN is available on cable.

BODY LANGUAGE

The Chinese don't touch each other as much as Westerners now do. Shaking hands is universal, and with friends both of the hands may be used and the handshake may last longer. Emphasis is on dignified and courteous behavior. Slouching and relaxing overtly may be regarded as rude.

A shake of the head means "no," and a nod means "yes." However, a nod may just signify understanding rather than agreement. A slight bow of the head is appropriate when introduced to someone for the first time, or from an inferior to a superior. As a congratulation or thanks, or to greet someone at New Year or some other festival, it is normal to clasp the hands and give a slight bow.

To beckon someone, don't do it the Western way. Raise your hand with the palm down, then move your fingers and hand toward you.

To thank someone for pouring a drink, drum your fingers a few times on the table, to signify bowing.

Thumbs up and thumbs down are used in the same way as in the West.

Cover your mouth when using a toothpick. It used to be thought unseemly for women to be seen with their mouths open and their teeth showing.

Pointing directly can be regarded as disrespectful. Another rude gesture that should be avoided is sticking your thumb between your index and middle fingers.

You may notice some Chinese people becoming red in the face after an alcoholic drink. This is because the enzymes in their bodies are not adapted to breaking down alcohol, so it has a more poisonous effect on their physiology. Many Chinese women swear off alcohol altogether, as they do not like this effect.

Laughter

Laughing can be misinterpreted by Westerners. Even if you are imparting serious news, such as the death of a member of your family, someone may laugh. It is not at all intended disrespectfully, but it is a way of covering up their awkwardness. If you fall over in the street, people are liable to laugh rather than help you up, which can be hurtful and puzzling. Women often cover their mouths when laughing, as a slightly embarrassed gesture.

SERVICES

Phone Booths

Many phone booths have disappeared since the advent of the ubiquitous cell phone. At the airport, Star Ferry, and other ferry terminals you can find public phone booths. You can also call from a post office, MTR station, or hotel lobby. For international calls, phone cards are useful and readily available, for example in 7-11 stores. Local calls are free from phones other than pay phones.

Cell Phones

Cell phones are now ubiquitous. It is easy to rent a cell phone. Hong Kong Telecom stores can be found throughout the territory; alternatively, most hotels will arrange it for you.

Internet

Internet is generally broadband, and there are many Internet cafés. You can get free Internet with your coffee in certain chain cafés.

Mail and Courier Services

Hong Kong's mail services are usually cheap, quick, and efficient. Letters take between three and five days to or from the U.S.A. and Europe. The General Post Office is close to the Star Ferry, and a list of other post offices can be found in the telephone directory in the first section Government Directory, under Post Office. Opening hours are Monday to Friday 8:00 a.m. to 6:00 p.m., and Saturday 8:00 a.m. to 2:00 p.m.

Major courier services as well as several local ones are available, and they are willing to pick up from almost anywhere in the city. Many MTR stations (such as Central) have DHL branches.

CONCLUSION

Hong Kong is an exceptional place, and is in the forefront of modern technology and business. Visitors marvel at its breathtaking location, its amazing buildings, its exciting shopping, and its fine dining. Business visitors will find not only the people engaged in business but also the government and banks approachable and cooperative. In terms of human achievement in the past fifty years, Hong Kong is probably the most extraordinary few square miles on the planet.

Further Reading

Travel Guides

Fallon, Steve, et al. *Lonely Planet Hong Kong & Macau: City Guide.* Melbourne/Oakland/London/Paris: Lonely Planet Publications, 2004.

Brown, Jules, et al. *The Rough Guide to Hong Kong and Macau.* London: Rough Guides, 2002.

Scott Rutherford (ed.) *Hong Kong Insight Guide.* Hong Kong: Insight Guides, 2003.

Art and Architecture

Morris, Jan. *Building Hong Kong.* Hong Kong: FormAsia, 1995.

Moss, Peter. *Hong Kong Style.* Hong Kong: FormAsia, 2000.

Politics and History

Fenby, Jonathan. *Dealing with the Dragon: A Year in the New Hong Kong.* New York: Time Warner Paperbacks, 2004.

Snow, Philip. *The Fall of Hong Kong: Britain, China and the Japanese Occupation.* New Haven, Conn. and London: Yale University Press, 2003.

Morris, Jan. *Hong Kong: Epilogue to an Empire.* London: Penguin Books, 1989.

Pullinger, Jackie, and Andrew Quicke. *Chasing the Dragon.* Hong Kong: Servant Ministries, reprinted 2004.

Moss, Peter. *Hong Kong Handover: Signed, Sealed & Delivered.* Hong Kong: FormAsia, 1999.

Cameron, Nigel, et al. *The Hong Kong Collection: Memorabilia of a Colonial Era.* Hong Kong: FormAsia, 1999.

Loh, Christine (Ed.). *Building Democracy: Creating Good Government for Hong Kong* (Civic Exchange Guides). Hong Kong: Hong Kong University Press, 2003.

Language

Mandarin Chinese. A Complete Course. New York: Living Language, 2006.

Business

Lethbridge, David G. (Ed.), et al. *The Business Environment in Hong Kong.* Hong Kong: Oxford University Press (China), 2000.

Shopping

Gershman, Suzy. *Born to Shop / Hong Kong, Shanghai & Beijing.* Ontario: John Wiley & Sons, 2003.

culture smart! hong kong

Index